COLLINS CONCISE GUIDE TO
THE FOOTPATHS
OF BRITAIN

COLLINS CONCISE GUIDE TO
THE FOOTPATHS OF BRITAIN

Michael Marriott

Willow Books
Collins
8 Grafton Street, London
1983

© Quintet Publishing Limited 1983

Willow Books
William Collins Sons & Co Ltd
London · Glasgow · Sydney
Auckland ·Toronto · Johannesburg

First published in Great Britain 1983

Marriott, Michael
Collins concise guide to the footpaths of Britain.
1. Trails – Great Britain – Guide-books
2. Great Britain – Description and travel – 1971
   – Guide-books
I. Title
914.1′04857 DA632

ISBN 0 00 218009 X

Designed and produced by
Quintet Publishing Limited, London

Editorial Director	Clare Howell
Editor	Christopher Pick
Art Editor	Christopher White
Designers	Mike Rose Robert Lamb
	Rose & Lamb Design
	Partnership
Illustrations	Sue Rose
Cartographer	Oxford Cartographers Limited

Phototypeset by
Hugh Wilson Typesetting, Norwich

Illustrations originated by
East Anglian Engraving Ltd, Norwich

Printed and bound in Italy by L.E.G.O. Vicenza

Contents

Introduction

A vast network of footpaths in Britain, covering over 100,000 miles, offers the walker an enormous choice of terrain and landscape. There is also a long and well-developed tradition of walking here. Many tracks date back to at least the Middle Ages, and some many centuries earlier still, their existence safeguarded in law (although vigilance remains necessary to ensure their preservation). Other paths are new creations, products of the late 20th-century leisure explosion and of the still vigorous enthusiasm for rambling.

This book represents a personal selection of the best walks in Britain. The basis of the choice, then, is personal experience, the result of more than thirty years of walking and writing about walking, plus the recommendations of Local Authorities and Tourist Boards. Here a word of thanks is due to all those who supplied information and answered queries; and to all those involved in establishing, maintaining and waymarking the footpaths.

The Collins Concise Guide to the Footpaths of Britain is aimed primarily at those who are just discovering or rediscovering the rewarding joy of walking for leisure. This is essentially a compact and practical reference book which can be consulted at a glance by walker and traveller alike, enabling them to assess the potential of any given walking area. The aim has been to give as wide and balanced a selection of walks as possible.

The organization of the book is simple: divided into six

broad geographical regions – the South, the West Country, the Midlands and East Anglia, Wales and the Borders, the North and Scotland. Each section commences with an account of the major long-distance paths. These routes, planned by the Countryside Commission, are some of Britain's most interesting, challenging and dramatic walks. Some – such as the Pennine Way – are for the experienced and practised walker. Others – the South Downs Way, for instance – can be tackled by anyone. Although not strictly long-distance paths, two major routes around urban conurbations – the West Midland Way and the London Countryway – are included here.

Each region then moves on to a county-by-county gazetteer of walks. Where they exist, the so-called recreational paths are described first. These waymarked routes, planned and maintained by the leisure and recreation departments of County Councils, vary considerably in length and difficulty. On the whole, though, they are shorter and easier than the long-distance paths. But they still represent the best in local walking through characteristic countryside and places of local interest. Finally, a wide selection of short walks from all parts of each county is provided.

The maps in the guide are intended to enable the reader to locate the position of the footpaths and towns mentioned in the text. Ordnance Survey map numbers are supplied in all cases for more detailed reference.

Michael Marriott

Equipment

In perfect weather it is obviously possible to walk many of the long-distance footpaths in ordinary clothes – but not in comfort or even in safety. The sterner the landscape, the more serious the potential weather, and the more essential the appropriate clothing and equipment. Even in summer the weather conditions on hills and moors can be unpredictable, while in winter the most gentle hills can become killers. At all times of the year the threat of exposure or hypothermia is a potential hazard for those who are not properly equipped, and can be fatal. Some of the basic clothing and equipment necessary for distance-walking in Britain is illustrated below, together with suggestions for backpacking. For the majority of short walks and strolls listed in the book the only equipment needed, apart from a map, will be sensible and comfortable footwear and a waterproof.

Mountain walking boots should be tought but flexible. A patterned Vibram sole is essential.

The new lightweight walking boots made of fabric and leather are excellent in most conditions. A special sole with cleats and studs prevents clogging.

Gaiters, made of canvas or nylon, help to prevent wet feet and are useful when negotiating bogs and mud.

Clothing should provide warmth and protection but should be light in weight and comfortable so that movement is not restricted. Waterproofs should also be windproof, with welded seams, storm cuffs and collar, hood, and protected zip; Derby tweed breeches are the best choice (left). A duvet jacket with a special fibre filling gives maximum insulation without extra weight (below).

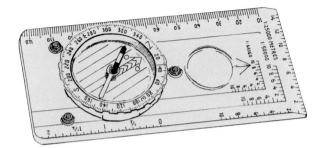

A compass is a vital piece of equipment – but you must know how to use it. The Silva orienteering compass is a good choice.

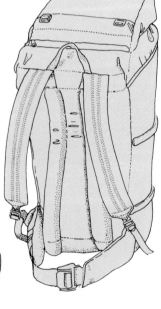

Rucksacks should be chosen with care to ensure a perfect fit. The integral frame should be contoured to the back for maximum comfort and for stability when scrambling or climbing. The larger types have a padded hip belt and shoulder straps.

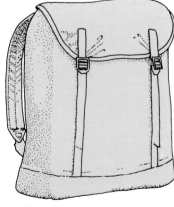

A small day sack is ideal for carrying the spare clothing, food, and map that will be needed on a short expedition.

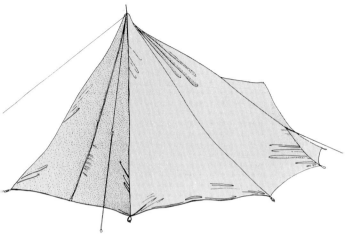

The new solo tents are ultra-lightweight (less than 3lb) yet spacious and pack extremely small, ,making them ideal for the backpacker.

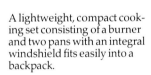

A lightweight, compact cooking set consisting of a burner and two pans with an integral windshield fits easily into a backpack.

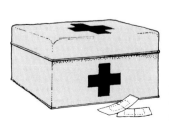

It is a sensible precaution to carry a small, lightweight first aid kit in case of emergencies.

11

Practical Information

The Country Code

Walkers should abide by the Country Code. Its rules are few and simple, and by observing them rigidly we can all help to preserve the countryside and an atmosphere of trust between town and country dwellers.

Guard against all risk of fire

Fasten all gates

Keep dogs under control

Keep to rights of way across farmland

Avoid damaging fences, hedges, and walls

Leave no litter

Safeguard water supplies

Protect wildlife, plants, and trees

Go carefully on country roads

Respect the life of the countryside

The Walker and the Law

● There are over 100 000 miles of public footpaths in Britain which are legally accessible to the walker. If the path is also a bridleway, you may ride a horse or cycle along it.

● You are only entitled to walk on the footpath or bridleway, not on adjacent land. Even in remote country you do not have the right to camp, light fires, pick flowers, or leave rubbish. This applies to fells and moorland, and is especially important in farmland and forests.

● Close all farm gates and keep dogs under control.

● If a marked path passes through a field of corn you are entitled to follow it, but make sure you do as little damage as possible.

● Take adequate care if a footpath crosses land grazed by bulls. Keep away from the animals and do not startle them by sudden noises or movements.

Safety in the Hills

● Do not walk alone until you are sufficiently experienced and confident. Know your own limitations – and adhere to them.

● Do not go into new terrain unprepared. Plan each expedition adequately with map and compass. Find out the best access and escape routes.

● It is advisable to walk in company. Three is a good number: if an emergency arises, one person can go for help while the other stays with the injured person.

● Err on the side of caution when planning a walk, in terms of both distance and weather conditions. Remember that the weather can change rapidly at high altitudes.

● Always leave word of your destination and intended route before setting out into the hills. If you cannot inform someone at your base, then even a note attached to the windscreen of your car will do.

● Make sure you carry emergency survival gear: extra warm clothing, quick-energy foods (e.g. chocolate), means of making a hot drink, a first-aid kit, whistle, and torch.

● Memorize the recognized distress signal: six long flashes or six long whistle blasts in quick succession, followed by a pause of one minute.

● If you get into a difficult situation, the thing is not to panic. Stop, think, then take appropriate action. Above all, do not rush down the mountain –this could get you into even more trouble. Stay put, find shelter if you can, keep warm, and wait for help to come.

Key to maps

○ ●	Towns or villages	●	Places of interest
⌷	Castles	=	River crossings
+	Churches or cathedrals	⊤⊤⊤⊤⊤	Canals
▲	Heights in feet	●●●●●	Recognized walks

The South

In many ways, southern England is ideal walking country. The going is always easy, the landscape varied and pleasant. Even the newest walker soon gains a sense of achievement, without risk from the weather or exhaustion from switchback slopes.

Those who come to know the region on foot soon recognize the richness and variety of the land. In the east, Kent and Essex, there are wide skies and flatland walks. There is excellent hill-walking everywhere: on the North, South and Berkshire Downs, through the Chilterns and, in Oxfordshire, on the fringes of the Cotswolds. Woodland and forest, lush farming country, riverside and canal-bank walks: all are within easy reach of the capital and other large population centres and make for ideal day and weekend expeditions.

The three long-distance paths – the North and South Downs Ways and the Ridgeway Path – have good claim to

1   Kent
2   East Sussex
3   West Sussex
4   Surrey
5   Hampshire
6   Isle of Wight
7   Berkshire
8   Oxfordshire
9   Buckinghamshire
10 Bedfordshire
11 Hertfordshire
12 Essex
13 Greater London

be the walking highlights of the south. But there are many other worthwhile routes, in particular the London Countryway, which circles the capital on astonishingly deserted paths. Here the characteristic sounds are not, as one might have expected, the hum of a great city, or even of its outer suburbs, but birdsong and other quiet noises of the deep countryside.

Everywhere within these twelve counties there are distinctive and enjoyable walks of every length.

Practical Points on Downland Walking

● Chalk tracks, particularly those which are much walked and peppered with protruding flints, are hard on the feet during long, dry spells. Even though contours are relatively gentle do not be too ambitious when planning your daily distance: 12 miles is a reasonable distance for beginners carrying a pack.

● In wet weather, chalk surfaces can be very slippery and sometimes deceptively treacherous on sharp inclines. Make sure you wear correct walking boots with non-slip soles.

● Many downland long-distance paths are also bridleways which may become very muddy after prolonged rain. It is usually possible to avoid the worst by picking your way, but this is time-consuming. Allow for such hold-ups and carry dry socks in your pack.

● Because of sheer numbers, it is advisable to make prior overnight arrangements along all recognized downland routes, especially in summer.

● Backpacking adds a new dimension of independence to a long-distance excursion. Make sure your load is lightweight, and always seek permission before pitching for the night.

THE SOUTH

The North Downs Way

Essential Information

Length: 140 miles, from Farnham (Surrey) to Dover (Kent); alternative routes from Wye to Dover run above Folkestone and through Canterbury
Going: easy, with a few harder stretches where the Way is not well defined
Terrain: chalk ridges of the North Downs giving way to undulating country in the Kentish Weald
OS maps: 178, 179, 186, 187, 188, 189

The North Downs Way runs along the top of the Surrey and Kent downs, near the suburban fringes of London. Its accessibility makes parts well trodden at weekends and in summer, although even then many sections are deserted. The going is as easy as the access. There are many delightful spots to enjoy and it is ideal for family outings. The Way is rich in history, coinciding in places with the Pilgrim's Way, and has been trodden since the Middle Ages.

Farnham to Dorking: 26 miles

The Way begins in the valley of the River Mole, just south of Farnham. Along the towpath at first, it rises to Crooksbury Hill near Seale and runs over Puttenham Common. From here a well-defined track goes through woodland, and then there is road walking through Compton. Next the Pilgrims Way is joined – bring a copy of *Canterbury Tales* – and the path continues to Guildford, where the fine cathedral and old Guildhall are worth a visit.

Towards Dorking the Way is beautiful and easy. The climb up Albury Downs brings good views from Newlands Corner (usually crowded in summer).

Map:

Mole valley ·○Farnham
Crooksbury Hill ▲
534 ○ Seale
Puttenham Common ·
Compton ○ ·
† ·○Guildford
Albury Downs ·. Newlands Corner
· Netley Heath
· Ranmore Common
Dorking ○ ·= *River Mole*
▲ Box Hill 563
Reigate ○ ·▲Colley Hill 756
Redhill ○ ○· Merstham
Gravelly Hill 778 ·· · White Hill 723
▲ Botley Hill
· 874
Westerham ○·○ Tatsfield
Chartwell · · Chevening
Dunton Green · · Park
Sevenoaks ○ · ○ Otford
·○ Wrotham
N ▲ Hill 721

0   5   10
miles

Rochester ○·
Chatham ○·
Bluebell Hill ▲ ·

Charing ○·
Wye ○·
Hastingleigh ○· ·○Chilham
Stowting ○·▲584
Lympne ○ · ·○Canterbury
· †
Folkestone ○·
White Cliffs · ○Shepherdswell
Dover ·○

Newlands Corner.

16

A pretty bridleway runs through woods, across Netley Heath and on to Ranmore Common, from where the path descends to the River Mole, crossed on stepping-stones.

Dorking to Otford: 31 miles

The walk from Box Hill to Reigate is busy but lovely. Keep steadily east across Brockham and Betchworth Hills, climb down to cross Pebble Hill Road and up again to Colley Hill. This stretch can be heavy going.

Out of Merstham, the path runs briefly along the A23 before climbing White and Gravelly Hills, crossing four major roads. But the view at the top is fine. Running south of Woldingham to Botley Hill it enters Kent at Tatsfield and continues to Westerham. The bronze figure in the town centre is of Winston Churchill, who lived in nearby Chartwell. There is pleasant walking around Chevening Park. The Way now descends to Dunton Green and crosses the Darent Valley to Otford.

Otford to Wye: 38 miles

The Way climbs to the rim of the Downs along a wooded scarp, then crosses the A21 at Wrotham. From Wrotham Hill there are good views over the Weald, and the path again follows the Pilgrim's Way to Rochester. Leave the traffic and climb up Wouldham Down and Bluebell Hill. A 13-mile stretch leads to Charing, with 18th-century timbered houses. The Way from here is delightful, a quiet path through apple orchards to Wye.

Wye to Dover: 27 miles

The Way divides here. The northern loop runs to Chilham,

Canterbury Cathedral.

where there is a fine Tudor square and a 15th-century castle with a Battle of Britain Museum. A splendid stretch over high ridge hills culminates in Canterbury. Rest here a while and enjoy this historic city. Especially in apple blossom time, the walk from Canterbury to Dover proves that Kent is the garden of England. On the last stretch, from Shepherdswell, you follow the old Roman road to Dover.

Wye to Dover: 18 miles

The shorter path to Dover begins by climbing to the ridge of the Downs above Hastingleigh before dropping to Stowting. It is good walking over Cheriton, Cherry Garden, Castle, Round and Sugarloaf Hills above Folkestone. From there to Dover the Way runs along the famous white cliffs: look for France on a clear day. The end is at the dramatic Shakespeare Cliff above the town and near the castle.

The South Downs Way

Essential Information

Length: 80 miles, from Eastbourne (Sussex) to the Sussex-Hampshire border near Petersfield
Going: easy
Terrain: chiefly ridge-walking along the South Downs; a few lowland stretches and numerous ascents and descents
OS maps: 197, 198, 199

The South Downs Way winds over downs, into green river valleys and through picturesque villages. For the most part it follows the ridge of the South Downs over an easy blend of flint and chalk. Quick access to villages and resorts makes the Way a good family walk, and it also provides long stretches of easy solitude.

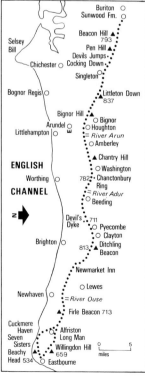

Eastbourne to Alfriston: 11 miles

The Way begins with a spectacular stretch of coastal walking. A steep climb from Eastbourne to the promontory of Beachy Head is rewarded with an exhilarating seascape across the Seven Sisters cliffs. Then the Way turns inland to Alfriston via Cuckmere Haven and Friston Forest, Westdean and Litlington, which has one of the smallest churches in England.

Alfriston has a number of old buildings, including a 14th-century clergy house. It is also the junction with the alternative path from Eastbourne. For a less bracing route, walkers can take the bridleway from Eastbourne inland to Wilmington Hill, past the Long Man of Wilmington, a chalk figure, 31 feet high, carved into the hill and believed to date from the 6th century.

Alfriston to Beeding: 32 miles

The path from Alfriston rises to Firle Beacon, with its huge barrow and fine views, before descending to the Ouse Valley, Southease and on to Newmarket Inn. Between Newmarket Inn and Beeding (17 miles) there is wooded and downland scenery. On Ditchling Beacon, the Weald stretches out below, the path continuing west to Devil's Dyke via the Jack and Jill windmills at Clayton. Now comes the descent to Pyecombe, where shepherds crooks were made in the old forge. Between Pyecombe and Devil's Dyke there is a magnificent view west towards Chanctonbury Ring. The Dyke is said to be part of a ditch dug by the devil inland to flood the

Chanctonbury Ring.

churches of the Weald. At Beeding Hill you will see the signpost erected by the Society of Sussex Downsmen to commemorate their Diamond Jubilee in 1973.

Beeding to Houghton: 15 miles

From Beeding the Way crosses the River Adur, strikes north to Bramber and Upper Beeding and continues across the rim of Annington Hill, where there is good escarpment walking. After farmland, you finally arrive at Chanctonbury Ring, an Iron Age earthwork encircling a beechwood. Now a flint track leads to Chantry Hill and on to Amberley Mount above the Arun Valley. The path falls to the river, where you are only 3 miles from Arundel with its castle and 1,100-acre park.

Houghton to Buriton: 22 miles

From the river climb to Houghton, which has a 13th-century church, over Bury and Westburton Hills to the heights above Bignor. This village is well worth a detour, for it has one of the largest Roman villas in Britain, with fine mosaic floors. After Bignor the Way becomes more wooded, the ground stony, and there is a fairly stiff climb through fields to Littleton Down, at 837 feet the highest point of the walk.

You are now almost on the last stretch, and the going is becoming easier and more enclosed, wooded, with clay, not chalk, underfoot. The woods continue past Singleton – which you should visit as there is a fascinating open-air museum with a magnificent collection of reconstructed historic buildings – and then the landscape opens out just before Cocking Down. Enjoy the views, with Chichester Harbour and the cathedral just visible. A little further on are the Devil's Jumps, Bronze Age burial mounds. The Way crosses woodland, goes up Pen Hill and down again and winds round Beacon Hill. The end, at Sunwood farm on the Hampshire border, is now in sight, but most walkers will probably want to continue to a well-earned drink in Buriton village.

19

The Ridgeway Path

Essential Information

Length: 85 miles, from East Kennett near Marlborough (Wiltshire), to Ivinghoe Beacon (Hertfordshire)

Going: easy

Terrain: chalk downland ridges on the western half, wooded hill country in the eastern sections; a number of ascents and descents

OS maps: 165, 173, 174, 175

Two of England's most ancient routes – the Great Ridgeway and the Icknield Way – form the basis of the modern Ridgeway Path. It runs along downland and through the wooded Chilterns from East Kennett in Wiltshire to Ivinghoe Beacon in Hertfordshire. It can be completed in a week and is a realistic challenge for aspiring walkers. The route is rich in historic remains, beautiful scenery and excellent walking.

East Kennett to Ogbourne: 10 miles

The Path begins at the foot of Overton Hill near the A4. Before setting off, visit the ancient barrow at West Kennet and Bronze Age stone circle at Avebury. The Path climbs to Overton Hill, Marlborough Downs and Hackpen Hill, then descends a lofty scarp and rises again to the Iron Age hill fort of Barbury Castle. A south turn along the chalk scarp of Smeathes Ridge leads to the thatched village of Ogbourne.

Ogbourne to Letcombe Bassett: 18 miles

The River Og is crossed at Southend, and the Path rises to 600 feet – heavy going in wet weather – before reaching Round Hill Down. The walk through Iron Age earthworks brings views of the Cotswolds in the distance and Liddington Castle in the foreground. The

Map locations:

West Kennet A4
892
Hackpen Hill
Barbury Castle
Marlborough
Southend — Ogbourne
Liddington
910 castle
Charlbury Hill
Lambourn
Wayland's Smithy
White Horse Hill — 856
Newbury
Letcombe Bassett
Segsbury Camp — Wantage
Grim's Ditch
Scutchamer Knob
Compton Downs
Lowbury Hill
614 — Abingdon
Streatley
Goring — River Thames
North Stoke
Nuffield
Watlington
835
Henley
Thame
Chinnor
Bledlow Great Wood
Princes Risborough
Pulpit Hill 813
Chequers
Coombe Hill
852
Wendover
Halton Wood — 876
Tring
Grand Union Canal =
Pitstone Hill
Ivinghoe
Beacon 756

0   5
miles

Wayland's Smithy.

The White Horse, Uffington.

next stretch, after Shepherds Rest Inn, is lovely farm country over Fox and Charlbury Hills, rising to 800 feet at Bishopstone. Two miles further on is Wayland's Smithy, a Neolithic chambered long barrow thought to have been built at least 4,500 years ago. The next section brings dramatic walking with panoramic views, and the celebrated chalk hill-figure, the White Horse of Uffington (365 feet long), Dragon Hill and the Manger, a huge geological gouge in the earth. Below the Path lies the village of Letcombe Bassett.

Letcombe Bassett to Streatley: 14 miles

This stretch has more views, over Didcot power station, Harwell and beyond, and Grims Ditch, an 8th-century boundary mark, runs nearby. The way is wide and green, then wooded before Scutchamer Knob, a Saxon barrow on the Oxfordshire-Berkshire border. Dropping near Harwell and down Compton Downs, the Path is less well defined. It is lovely country to Streatley and the Goring Gap, the halfway point of the walk.

Streatley to Bledlow: 21 miles

It is open and beautiful here, perfect walking country. The Path follows the Thames to South and North Stoke, then strikes off to Nuffield, where William Morris, the car magnate, is buried, and Watlington, a good stop for refreshment. Onwards the route is partly wooded, opening out with cement works before Chinnor. But Bledlow Great Wood and views of Princes Risborough make this stretch worthwhile.

Bledlow to Ivinghoe Beacon: 22 miles

The Path rounds Princes Risborough, with its thatched and timbered cottages, climbs Whiteleaf Hill and runs along Pulpit Hill. There is an interesting glimpse of the prime minister's official country residence as the Path passes through the grounds of Chequers. The land is rich and wooded, and the Path rises and falls over Lodge, Coombe (at 850 feet one of the highest points of the Chilterns) and Bacombe Hills, and on down to Wendover.

From Wendover to Ivinghoe the Path makes a wide southerly sweep round Tring and the Grand Union Canal. Then comes the final northward climb over Pitstone Hill with its 17th-century windmill and up to Ivinghoe Beacon. The fine landscape and grand views make a fitting end to the walk.

The windmill on Pitstone Hill.

The London Countryway

Essential Information

Length: 205 miles, in a circular route around London

Going: easy, across field paths and hills

Terrain: hilly along the North Downs in the south and the Chilterns in the north-west; otherwise a mixture of undulating and flat land, especially near the Thames

OS maps: 165, 166, 167, 175, 177, 186, 187, 188

The London Countryway completely surrounds London. But on most stretches the walker can scarcely sense the presence of the capital city. True, main roads have to be crossed and towns and villages skirted more often than on other long-distance walks. But in the countryside itself London might be 100 miles away rather than a quarter of that distance, (at its nearest point, the way is 13 miles from Charing Cross, at its furthest 31).

Its proximity to London makes the walk ideal for day or weekend outings and for family expeditions. There is a variety of scenery to enjoy, and the path (which runs along public footpaths and is not waymarked) passes near many places of historic interest.

St Albans to Theydon Bois: 33 miles

St Albans is one of the most important towns on the Way, and there are the cathedral and the Roman remains to see. The path skirts Hatfield, where the Cecil family home at Hatfield House is worth a visit, runs through North Mimms, Brookmans Park and then across London clay (liable to turn to mud) to Wormley Wood, where the route is rather complicated. The next target is Broxbourne, after which there is a section along the Lea Valley to Waltham Abbey and then through Epping Forest to Theydon Bois. The latter was once a Norman forest, now encroached upon by the growth of London suburbs.

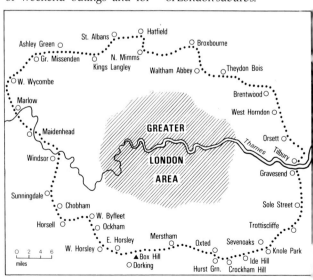

Theydon Bois to Tilbury: 31 miles

Paths across the pleasant Essex uplands lead to Stapleford Tawney, over the River Roding, round Brentwood through Thorndon Park and on to West Horndon. The churches in this area are especially interesting and worth a visit. Then it is across the flat Essex coastal plain to Orsett and East Tilbury. The final stretch is fascinating: across marshland and then along the river from Coalhouse Fort, built in 1869, to Tilbury Fort and Tilbury itself, where there is a ferry across the Thames.

Gravesend to Hurst Green: 35½ miles

From Gravesend the path follows the Wealdway (see page 24) to Sole Street and then runs along the North Kent Downs, across the Pilgrim's Way, to Trottiscliffe and Platt. This is fine country, apple-orchard land. Now there are superb views over the Weald as the path runs through the grounds of Fairlawne House and Ightham Mote and on to Knole Park and Ide Hill. A section in sandstone country then brings the walker across Crockham Hill Common to Hurst Green.

Hurst Green to West Byfleet: 35½ miles

Oxted and Tandridge Hill are landmarks, and then there is a stretch shared with the North Downs Way through Merstham and Box Hill to Hackhurst Downs. The Countryway now turns north-west to East and West Horsley, across Ockham Common and Wisley Common and along the Wey Navigation to West Byfleet.

West Byfleet to West Wycombe: 31 miles

Two large commons, Horsell and Chobham, bring the walker to Sunningdale, and there is more fine walking across Windsor Park to Windsor. Then there is a Thames-side stretch, 7 miles through Maidenhead to Boulter's Lock. Cookham Moor, Winter Hill (note the good views of the Chilterns ahead) and Marlow are next, followed by the first Chilterns stretch, to West Wycombe.

West Wycombe to St Albans: 30½ miles

This is true Chilterns country, with no less than four ascents and descents before Great Missenden. Then the path runs across country to Ashley Green and on to Kings Langley. The Chilterns are behind now, and the final leg is through easy country to St Albans.

From Box Hill there are fine views over the Mole Valley.

23

Kent

The North Downs Way runs the length of the county and provides many excellent walks. The London Countryway (see pages 22-23) also runs through North Kent.

The Wealdway

Essential Information

Length: 80 miles, from Gravesend to Eastbourne (Sussex)
Going: easy
OS maps: 188, 198,

This is a pleasant path through the Kent and Sussex Weald from the Thames estuary to the Channel coast. Out of Gravesend, Sole Street is the first place of interest; there is a Tudor 'yeoman's house' here. Then comes Luddesdown and a North Downs stretch to Trott-iscliffe, West Peckham and an easy walk across the Medway Valley to Barnes Street. Oast houses and orchards, those typical signs of the Kent land-scape, abound here. The path into Tonbridge (28 miles) is along the Medway, and then there is pleasant walking to Ashdown Forest, across the Sussex border. The next object-ive is Uckfield (55 miles), fol-lowed by farmland stretches through the Cuckmere Valley towards the South Downs and Eastbourne.

The Saxon Shore Way

Essential Information

Length: 140 miles, from Gravesend to Rye (Sussex)
Going: easy
OS maps: 177, 178, 179, 189

Typical Kentish landscape.

This is a most unusual walk, hugging practically the whole Kentish coastline. Its name recalls the 5th century AD, when a chain of forts was built along the south-east coast to guard England against Saxon invaders. And, in the first sections of the Way at least, the military theme continues, for soon after the start at Gravesend the walker passes two 19th-century Thames forts. Some 12 miles further on the Way reaches Upnor Castle, whose guns drove off Dutch invaders in 1697. Then comes Rochester, where the path crosses the Medway, and a stretch along the sea wall, across reclaimed marshland and up and down creeks towards Kingsferry Bridge (37 miles). Then it is along The Swale through Sittingbourne to Faversham and Whitstable. After Herne Bay and Reculver, the Way cuts behind the Isle of Thanet to Sandwich (89 miles), following the course of ancient waterways now silted up. A brisk cliff walk leads to Dover, Folkestone and Hythe (119 miles). The last stretch is along the Royal Military Canal into Rye. The Canal was commissioned during the Napoleonic Wars to safeguard Romney Marsh, but was never finished.

Suggested Walking Areas

● Trottiscliffe

The Trosley Country Park on the North Downs offers three fine walks:
The Coldrum Trail (6 miles)
The Trosley Ramble (3½ miles)
The Harvel Hike (7 miles)

● Tunbridge Wells

This charming spa town is the starting-point for a number of circular walks:
Pantiles to Rusthall Common (4 miles)
Town Hall to Hawkenbury (5½ miles)
Pantiles to Hawkenbury (3½ miles)
Tunbridge Wells Common to Rusthall (5 miles)
Pantiles to High Rocks (5½ miles)

● West Malling

From Manor Country Park, just outside West Malling, there are four pleasant circular walks:
St Leonard's Walk (4 miles) to Ryarsh Church
The Quintain Walk to Offham (4 miles)
The Millstream Walk (3¼ miles) to East Malling
Woods Meadows Walk (3 miles) to Leybourne Wood

● The White Cliffs of Dover

Two circular routes along the Cliffs are:
St Margaret's Down (5½ miles), from St Margaret's Bay along the coast to Kingsdown, returning inland.
The South Foreland (6½ miles), from the Langdon Cliffs picnic site north of Dover along the coast to St Margaret's and back inland.

OS maps: 177, 178, 179, 188, 189

Surrey

The North Downs Way (see pages 16-17) passes through the north of the county. The sections near Puttenham, and around Ranmore Common and Box Hill, are particularly good walks.

The Greensand Way

Essential Information

Length: 55 miles, from Haslemere to Limpsfield
Going: easy
OS map: 187

This path runs along the greensand escarpment of the Surrey Hills. It is a pleasant and easy walk over well-drained land, and despite the proximity of major towns, this is everywhere a peaceful route. Starting from the Hindhead massif, the Way passes the famous Devil's Punchbowl at Hindhead and then runs through the Hambledon Hills. Other natural features are Winterfold Hill, Pitch Hill, Holmbury Hill, where there is an ancient earthwork, Leith Hill, Surrey's highest, Earlswood Common and Limpsfield Chart. From the Way's end it is a short walk over the Kent border into Westerham. There are no less than five link paths to the North Downs Way (between 1½ and 6 miles) to the north.

The Wey-South Path

Essential Information

Length: 36 miles, from Guildford to Amberley (Sussex)
Going: easy
OS maps: 186, 187, 197

The Wey-South Path is an attractive connecting route between the North and South Downs Ways (see pages 16-19). For almost two-thirds of the distance the Path runs along the Wey and Arun Canal. These stretches are of especial interest as the Canal, at present being restored, was an important link in its early 19th-century heyday between the Thames and the south coast. There is a variety of landscape on the walk: the Surrey Hills in the north, woodland and the Weald, the valley of the upper Arun, marshlands and the chalk ridge of the South Downs. The Way follows a combination of towpaths, footpaths, minor roads and disused railway track through Stonebridge, Bramley and Elmbridge to Fast Bridge, from where a woodland path leads to the locks at Sidney Wood and then to the junction of the Wey and Arun at Newbridge. Water meadows and open pasture bring the walker to the end of

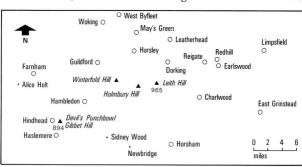

the Canal at Pallingham Lock, from where the Path continues near the Arun to Amberley.

Suggested Walking Areas

● Abinger Ranmore

A high forest walk offers views of the Weald and Leith Hill.

● Alice Holt Forest

There is a variety of forest trails through the forest, once a royal hunting-ground, which lies on the Hampshire border 4 miles south of Farnham.

● Devil's Punchbowl

The Punchbowl is a deep combe beneath Gibbet Hill, Hindhead. A 2½-mile nature trail begins on the southern rim of the valley.

● Gibbet Hill

Gibbet Hill, 894 feet high, is a good walk from Hindhead, the views making the climb worthwhile. A 2-mile nature trail begins from the car park on the A3.

● Horsley to Woking

This 11-mile walk passes through fine country. From Barnsworth Wood, especially beautiful at bluebell time, it runs to May's Green and Martyr's Green, the woods at Ockham Common and the open space of Wisley Common. (A detour here to the Royal Horticultural Society's gardens is well worth the time.) Before Ockham Mill follow the towpath of the Wey Navigation Canal for 1¼ miles to West Byfleet station. At West Byfleet join the Basingstoke Canal for the last 2 miles along the towpath to Woking.

View over Dorking.

● Mole Valley

The area between Dorking and Leatherhead is the centre for a number of good walks, both in Weald countryside and on the southside of the North Downs. Especially recommended circular routes are:
Friday Street to Leith Hill and Coldharbour (5½ miles)
Bookham, Polesden Lacey and Norbury Park (3¼ miles)
Brockham to Betchworth (2½ miles)
Norbury Park (2½ miles)
Dorking to Brockham (6 miles)
Dorking to Leatherhead follows the east bank of the River Mole in one direction (7½ miles), the west bank on the return (5½ miles)
Bucklands and the North Downs (3 miles)
Leatherhead to Staine Street and Mickleham (7 miles)
Leatherhead to Westhumble (6½ miles)
Leigh to Betchworth (8 miles)
Newdigate to Charlwood (7½ miles)
Walliswood and Oakwood Hill (3¼ miles)

● Witley Common

Just south-west of Milford, there are three nature trails over the heathland here.

OS maps: 176, 186, 187

Sussex

The South Downs Way (see pages 18-19) runs the length of the South Downs, from Eastbourne in the east to the Hampshire border in the west. Much of the Wealdway from Gravesend (Kent) to Eastbourne runs through Sussex (see page 24), as does the Wey South Path (page 26).

The Sussex Border Path

Essential Information

Length: 148 miles, from Thorney Island to Rye, plus a 37-mile link route from East Grinstead to Mile Oak, Southwick
Going: generally easy, but with a few difficult patches
OS maps: 186, 187, 188, 189, 197, 198, 199

This is a frontier route, following as nearly as possible the entire borders of Sussex. The start is at Thorney Island. The Path runs north along the border with Hampshire and then turns to go east and southeast along the Surrey and Kent borders. The Mid-Sussex link runs due south along the border between East and West Sussex.

The route begins with a circular walk round Thorney Island and then makes northwards from Emsworth (starting-point of the Wayfarers' Walk, see page 31) through pleasant country for the Downs. Once the Rother Valley is crossed, there is wooded country to Liphook. Then comes the ascent of Black Down and a section on high ground to Rudgwick (54½ miles). After passing near Gatwick Airport, the Path runs along the Worth Way into East Grinstead and then follows a rather unclear route across country to Cowden. There are good views of the North Downs here. Paths along the River Medway and then through sandstone country bring the walker to Boarshead (104½ miles). The final sections are through the Weald to Wadhurst, past the Bewl Bridge Reservoir to Union Street, through orchard country to Bodiam and then along the Rother towpath into Rye.

The Mid-Sussex link follows the Forest Way to Horsted Keynes, crosses the River Ouse

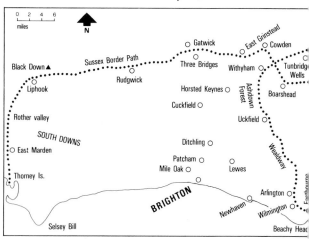

The Long Man, Wilmington.

and then Ditchling Common and finally climbs the Downs to Patcham, finishing at Mile Oak.

An additional 40-mile route through pleasant country links Rye with the start of the Path at Eastbourne.

Forest Way

Essential Information

Length: 9½ miles, from East Grinstead to Ashurst Junction
Going: easy
OS maps: 187, 188

This path runs along the track of a disused branch line opened in 1866 by the London, Brighton and South Coast Railway. Much of the walk is in pleasant woodland, and there are good views of Ashdown Forest. The Medway water meadows are crossed to Withyham, and the end of the walk is at Ashurst Junction, just outside Groombridge. The walk can be extended on public footpaths into Tunbridge Wells (Kent).

Suggested Walking Areas

● Arlington

There is a pleasant 8½-mile walk from **Alfriston to Horsebridge** through the parish of Arlington. The countryside is delightful at all seasons.
Arlington Reservoir, three circular walks from 2 to 4 miles.
The Bluebell Walk is open for the first three weeks in May.

● Ashdown Forest

Here is impressive walking country rising to 700 feet. A 5-mile circular route through the forest starts at Nutley Windmill.

● Brighton

Stanmer Park and Ditchling Beacon (9 miles)
Patcham and Clayton circular (10½ miles)
Rottingdean and Woodingdean circular (7 miles)
Saltdean circular (10 miles)

29

● Cuckfield

There are 12 pleasant walks in and around Cuckfield, between 2 and 7 miles long, through the pleasant country near this pretty town.

● Eastbourne

Friston and East Dean circular (9 miles)
Willingdon and Jevington circular (4½ miles)
East Dean and Belle Toute circular (6 miles)

● East Marden

There is good walking through woodland and up on to the Downs near here. Kingley Vale, a nature reserve, and Bow Hill are especially attractive.

● Hastings

The Hastings Country Park, a fine 500-acre stretch of unspoilt coast, has five glen Trails, each about 2 miles long.

● Lewes

Lewes, Offham and Kingston circular (14 miles)
Glynde and Mount Caburn circular (3 miles)
Lewes, Kingston and Iford circular (8 miles)
Alfriston and Hobbs Heath circular (8 miles)

● Newhaven and Seaford

Denton and West Firle circular (10 miles)
Denton and Telscombe circular (13 miles)
Seaford and Bishopstone circular (7 miles)
Seaford Head circular (6 miles)

● Three Bridges

The Worth Way is a 6-mile path from Three Bridges to East Grinstead along the track of a disused railway line. The going may well be wet.

● Uckfield

Uckfield and Blackboys circular (13 miles)

● Wilmington

The **Wilmington Historical Walk** (4¾ miles) passes old mine workings, the Long Man of Wilmington, Wilmington Priory and a number of long barrows.

OS maps: 187, 188, 189, 197, 198, 199

The downs near Ditchling Beacon.

Hampshire

The Wayfarer's Walk

Essential Information

Length: 70 miles, from Emsworth to Inkpen Beacon
Going: easy
OS maps: 196, 185, 174

The Way combines footpaths, bridleways and green trackways to run from the Solent coast, through the heart of Hampshire to the chalk ridges of the Berkshire Downs. The Way starts at Emsworth Harbour with fine views of Hayling Island. Then it passes Langstone Harbour and the saltmarsh islands, through the Forest of Bere and Hambledon (note the Saxon church) to the Meon Valley and Droxford and its fine Georgian houses. The Way continues through Corhampton Forest to the prehistoric South Hampshire Ridgeway. Along the River Itchen the Way reaches Cheriton, then Tichborne, and then climbs Abbotstone Down and the chalk hills to Dummer. The last stretch is through Kingsclere and the Highclere Estate, finally running on ancient trackways to Inkpen Beacon, 954 feet above sea level.

The Solent Way

Essential Information

Length: 58 miles, from Emsworth, along the Solent and Spithead coastline to Milford-on-Sea near Lymington
Going: easy
OS maps: 174, 185, 196

Like the Wayfarer's Walk and the Sussex Border Path, the Solent Way starts at Emsworth on the Sussex border. It crosses

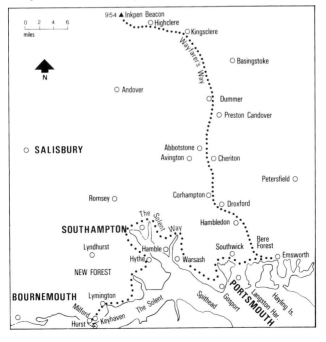

shingle beaches, waymarked country lanes, parts of the New Forest and makes use of four ferry crossings: Hurst Castle to Keyhaven, Hythe to Southampton, Hamble to Warsash and Gosport to Portsmouth. There are plenty of interesting sights along the route: castles at Hurst, near Lymington, and Southsea, and the harbours at Southampton, Gosport and Portsmouth. Above all, there is much for the naval historian: the Submarine Museum at Gosport, Nelson's *Victory* and most recently the *Mary Rose*.

Suggested Walking Areas

● Avington

There are three walks from this charming village in the Itchen Valley, to Martyr Worthy (2½ miles), Itchen Abbas (2½ miles) and Abbots Worthy (5 miles).

● The New Forest

The widest stretch of unenclosed land in southern England, the 145 square miles are a former royal hunting forest. The Forestry Commission has marked a wide variety of walks within the area. A particularly good day's walking is from Minehead to Burley and Holmsley. Douglas Firs, planted in 1860, make a spectacular setting for fine forest walking, starting from Bolderwood car park near Lyndhurst. The Brock Hill Walk and Tall Trees Walk start at Blackwater car park off the A35, west of Lyndhurst, and there are handsome conifer walks near Rhinefield House, along the Rhinefield Ornamental Drive.

● Southwick

The Southwick Estate has been the site of some fascinating history. The priory dates from 1133 and eight centuries later Eisenhower gave the final D-Day orders from Southwick House. There are three marked routes, two of 7½ miles and 4½ miles through back lanes from the car park, plus a shorter stroll from St James' Church.

● Queen Elizabeth Country Park

Three miles south of Petersfield, this 1,400-acre park of forest and downland offers a variety of walks on waymarked trails and footpaths.

OS maps: 174, 175, 184, 185, 186, 196

Emsworth Harbour.

Isle of Wight

Isle of Wight Coastal Path

Essential Information

Length: 60 miles, along the island's entire coastline

Going: easy

OS map: 196

This coastline path falls naturally into four sections of about 15 miles each.

The North-east section starts in East Cowes and passes Norris Castle, Queen Victoria's seaside home at Osborne and the Regency resort of Ryde, ending at Bembridge.

The South-east path passes through the resorts of Sandown, Shanklin and Ventnor, climbs to the island's highest point, St Boniface Down (787 feet), and runs along the 7-mile Undercliff, ending at St Catherine's Lighthouse.

The South-west section takes the walker through the various chines, all areas of great geological interest and on to fine views at Freshwater Bay and the coloured sands of Alum Bay.

The North-west path runs through the resorts of Totland and Yarmouth, Bouldnor Cliffs and Hamsted Ledge and ends at Cowes, famous for its regatta every August.

Freshwater and Tennyson Downs.

Suggested Walking Areas

● Seven long-distance trails

Over eighty miles of extremely walkable footpath and bridleway criss-cross the island. Seven long-distance trails form the main paths.

Tennyson Trail: Carisbrooke Castle to Alum Bay. 15 miles of downland, forest paths and sea views.

Worsley Trail: 15 miles from Shanklin Old Village to Brighstone Forest, passing through villages of historic interest.

Stenbury Trail: 10 miles through river valleys from Blackwater to Ventnor.

Nunwell Trail: 10 miles from Ryde to Sandown through varied countryside with interesting wildlife.

Bembridge Trail: 15 miles through historic villages from Shide to Bembridge.

Hamsted Trail: 8 miles of saltings and cliffs from Brook Bay to Hamsted Ledge.

Shepherd's Trail: 10 miles on high ground and through historic villages from Whitcombe Cross to Atherfield.

OS map: 196

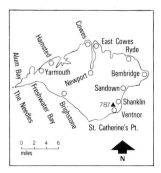

33

Berkshire

The Ridgeway Path (see pages 20-21) runs along the Berkshire/Oxfordshire border. The London Countryway (see pages 22-23) also runs through the east of the county.

Suggested Walking Areas

● Blackwater Valley

There are pleasant walks here, among them along Wellingtonia Avenue, planted in the late 19th century, and from Wokingham to Finchampstead Ridges and Ambarrow Hill (5 miles).

● Cookham

A fine Thames-side path leads from Cookham through watermeadows and then up to the top of Winter Hill. There are also pleasant walks along the river.

● Hungerford

The path to Walbury Hill and Combe Hamlet (4 miles) runs through Inkpen. After Gallows Down, it climbs Walbury Hill (974 feet), the highest point in the county, and runs along the Downs to Woodhay Down and Combe Hamlet.
The Kennet and Avon Canal flows through lush water meadows and provides easy, peaceful towpath walks. Access is best from Hungerford.

● Long Wittenham

A bracing walk leads from the village through Little Wittenham and Wittenham Wood to Wittenham Clumps, an ancient hill fort perched on a hilltop. The views stretch from the Vale of the White Horse to the Chilterns.

● Newbury

There is a pleasant walk to Snelsmore Common via the ruins of Donnington Castle.

● Wallingford

The 15-mile walk from Wallingford to Pangbourne is a fine expedition. From Wallingford the path runs through Goring Gap, where the Berkshire Downs and the Chilterns descend to the Thames, and on up the 500-foot Streatley Hill. The climb is steep, but the views superb. Between Goring and Pangbourne visit Basildon Park, a fine National Trust house with good walks in the extensive grounds.

OS maps: 165, 174, 175, 176

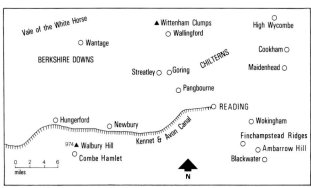

Oxfordshire

The Ridgeway Path (see pages 20-21) runs through the southern part of the country, offering splendid walks along the ridge of the Berkshire Downs.

The Oxfordshire Way

Essential Information

Length: 65 miles, from Henley-on-Thames to Bourton-on-the-Water (Gloucestershire)
Going: easy
OS maps: 163, 164, 174, 175

Oxfordshire Way, near Maidensgrove.

The Oxfordshire Way runs across Oxfordshire, linking the Chilterns and the Cotswolds and crossing a number of Thames tributaries, including the Thame, Ray, and Evenlode. From Henley the first target is Pyrton, via Stonor Hill and Christmas Common. Pyrton is a delightfully tiny and remote village, with a 17th-century manor house. Then come Tetsworth, Rycote (where there is a 15th-century chapel), Waterstock, Waterperry and Beckley (29 miles). A Roman road crossed Otmoor here, an an-

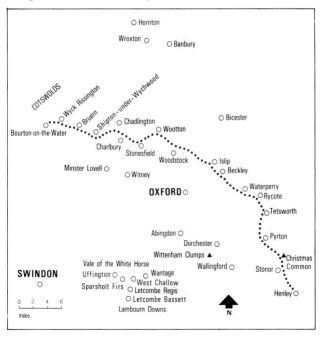

cient piece of fenland. After Islip, at the junction of the Ray and Cherwell Rivers, there is a series of beautiful Cotswold villages: Wootton, Stonesfield, Charlbury. Six miles of the Way here run along Akeman Street, the Roman road that runs from Cirencester to Alchester; the views along this stretch are magnificent. The Evenlode Valley brings the walker to Shipton-under-Wychwood and Bruern and then it is up on to the Cotswolds themselves, with wide views. A short walk through Wyck Rissington leads to Bourton-on-the-Water.

Suggested Walking Areas

● Banbury

The Giant's Cave Picnic Site, just outside Banbury, is the starting-point for a series of pleasant walks through farmland in the Upper Sor Valley, between 2½ and 5 miles long.

● Chadlington

A fine 2½-mile walk runs on the Chadlington Downs from the High Hawk Stone east to Spelsbury.

● Sparsholt Firs

There is an 8½-mile high downland walk from the car park on the B4001 Childrey to Lambourn road. The route runs along the Ridgeway, descends to Letcombe Bassett and climbs up again to Rats Hill and Red Barn.

● Vale of the White Horse

From Woolstone, 1 mile south of Uffington, there is a good 2½-mile walk with fine views of the chalk horse up to Uffington Castle and Wayland's Smithy on the Ridgeway Path.

● Wallingford

There are two circular walks from this historic town through the Thames Valley, to **Dorchester** (9 miles) and to **Wittenham Clumps** (8½ miles).

● Wantage

A 7-mile circular walk runs through the villages of Letcombe Regis and West Challow at the foot of the Downs.

● Witney

A 13-mile circular walk runs through the lovely Upper Windrush Valley, past the Chartist settlement near Charterville Allotments and through Minster Lovell.

● Wittenham Clumps

The starting-point for three overlapping walks is a coppice planted in the late 18th century and recently replanted with beech and other trees. The routes are via **Little Wittenham and Long Wittenham** (6½ miles), **Brightwell and Wittenham Woods** (5½ miles) and **Dorchester and the Thames towpath** (6 miles).

● Woodstock

There are miles of footpaths through the magnificent landscape of Blenheim Park, designed for the Duke of Marlborough by Capability Brown, often with stunning vistas of the Palace.

● Wroxton

The ironstone landscape of North Oxfordshire is the setting for the 9-mile circular walk from Wroxton, near Banbury, through Shennington and Hornton.

OS maps: 151, 152, 163, 164, 174

Buckinghamshire

The North Buckinghamshire Way

Essential Information

Length: 30 miles from Chequers Knapp on the Chiltern Ridgeway to Wolverton

Going: easy

OS Maps: 152, 165

Cottages in Little Missenden.

The Vale of Aylesbury is at the heart of this 30-mile waymarked footpath and part of it may be very wet and muddy during autumn and winter. Starting near the Prime Minister's country home at Chequers, the footpath moves downhill into Great Kimble and on to Bishopstone and Hartwell, all villages of considerable historical interest. Then it runs across fields and past farms to Waddesdon and the manor house, which is well worth a visit. From the village green at Quainton with its old market cross, windmill and almshouses there are splendid views over the Vale. The Way continues past Fulbrook Farm to East Claydon and the superb Claydon House. From Great Horwood with its many Georgian houses field tracks bring the walker to Nash and then the early medieval church at Whaddon and Whaddon Hall. City footpaths take the walker through a corner of Milton Keynes and on to Wolverton Cemetery. The walk may be extended to take in the Grand Union Canal, Fenny Stratford or the Canal Museum at Stoke Bruerne.

Suggested Walking Areas

● Burnham Beeches

There are numerous footpaths in this vast 60-acre beech forest in the Chilterns. The going may be wet. The best time to see the beeches is in spring and autumn.

● Chilterns

Footpaths criss-cross the Chilterns providing a variety of walks through beechwood and interesting villages such as the Missendens, and Chalfont St Giles.

● West Wycombe

Hellfire Club caves combine with West Wycombe village and the National Trust property at West Wycombe Park to provide a fine walk across woodland and green tracks.

OS maps: 152, 153, 165, 175, 176

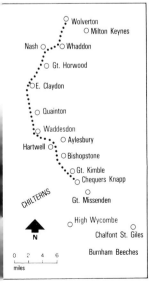

37

Bedfordshire

Suggested Walking Areas

● Bedford Riverside Walks

Six short walks along the banks of the Ouse as it passes through Bedford and Kempston.

● 2-hour circular walk from **Bromham Mill to Clapham**. Starts from the 18th-century mill with good views of the river and historic Bromham Bridge and passes the late medieval church of St Owen's.

● 2 hours of farm track walking, circling through countryside and taking in **Kempston Mill**.

● 2-hour meadowland walk from **Queen's Bridge to Kempston Mill** and back.

● ½-hour easy walk from **Bedford's** famous **Town Bridge** past St Paul's Church to **Prebend Street** and back.

● 1-hour circular walk along the **Embankment**, Bedford's riverside showpiece.

● 2-hour circular walk from **Longholme Way to Cardington Lock**, skirting the Priory Marina Park.

● Dunstable Downs

Magnificent views of the Vale of Aylesbury are to be had from the many footpaths that cross the Chilterns at their

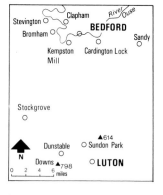

The eighteenth-century windmill at Stevington is still in working order.

highest point in the county. Interesting flora, gentle rolling countryside.

● Stevington Country Walk

1¾-mile walk along a disused railway line with superb views of the Ouse Valley. Visit historic Stevington Windmill after the walk.

● Stockgrove Country Park

A fascinating Nature Trail running through the Park along the Bedfordshire outcrop of Lower Greensand. There is wildfowl, and the woodland sections are rich in wild flowers.

● Sundon Hills

Several waymarked walks run through the proposed Sundon Hills Country Park, nearly 100 acres of the chalk escarpment and high grassland offering superb views of the mid-Bedfordshire countryside.

OS maps: 152, 153, 165, 166

Hertfordshire

A short section of the Ridge-way Path (see pages 20-21) and of the Harcamlow Way (see page 41) runs through the county.

Suggested Walking Areas

Ayot St Lawrence

There is a pleasant 7½-mile circular walk round Ayot St Lawrence on minor roads and field paths. From Shaw's Corner the path runs to Lamer House and Water End House, returning via Hunter's Bridge.

● Grand Union Canal

The towpath of the Grand Union Canal, which runs north/south through the county, makes a grand walk. The section from Watford north to Tring is especially recommended.

Hertford

The Cole Green Way is a 4-mile walk from Hertford to Cole Green along the track of a disused railway.

Icknield Way

The Icknield Way is the eastern part of the great ridge route that runs from Wessex north-east into East Anglia. The modern Ridgeway Path fol-lows its route as far as Ivinghoe Beacon, but the Way can also be walked further east. A par-ticularly good stretch is from the A6 north of Luton to Ickleford, north of Hitchin.

● Wheathampstead

Another railway walk, also of 4 miles, runs along the Ayot Greenway from Wheathamp-stead to Welwyn Garden City.

● Other circular walks in Hertfordshire include:

Brickendon, from Bayford Station to Highfield Wood (6 miles)
Little Gaddesden to Berkham-sted (8½ miles)
Rickmansworth to Sarratt Bottom (8 miles)
Chipperfield to Kings Langley (6 miles)
Old Knebworth to Codicote (6½ miles)
High Wych to Sawbridgeworth (7 miles)
Blakesware monastery to Stanstead Abbots (8½ miles)

OS maps: 153, 154, 165, 166, 167, 176

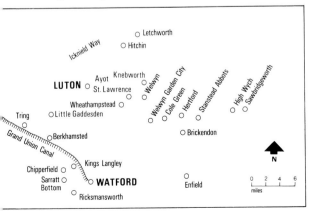

Essex

Epping Forest Centenary Walk

Essential Information

Length: 15 miles, from Manor Park station to Epping
Going: easy, sometimes boggy
OS maps: 167, 177

This path runs the full length of Epping Forest and offers walkers a marvellous chance to observe the forest's wild life and fauna. The route runs through Wanstead Flats and past Highams Park to the Epping Forest Museum at Chingford. Then it passes Connaught Water and runs through beech woods to end at Epping.

Three Forests Way

Essential Information

Length: 60 miles, to and from Loughton
Going: easy
OS maps: 166, 167

The three forests of the title are Epping, Hatfield and Hainault – once much larger than they are today, for the path is largely on open ground. Past earth works at Loughton Camp, the Way continues into the beech woods of Epping Forest to the village of Upshire, then on to Nazeing and Roydon. From Hatfield Forest waymarked paths pass through the lovely Roding Valley and past historic Chipping Norton. The return to Loughton is through Hainault Forest.

Essex Way

Essential Information

Length: 50 miles, from Epping to Dedham
Going: easy
OS maps: 167, 168, 177

Gently rolling open country makes a brisk pace possible on this easy route. There is historical interest at Greenstead where there is a Saxon church and Pleshey boasts an impressive Norman castle. Then at Cressing are the remains of the Knights Templars' first settlement in England. The walk concludes in Dedham.

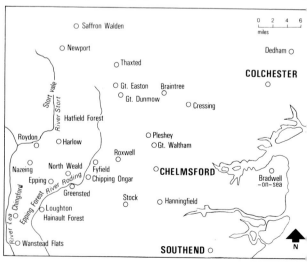

...ale, immortalized by Constable, and designated an Area ...Outstanding Natural Beauty, ...d at Dedham itself, with fine ...dor and Georgian houses.

...arcamlow Way

...ssential Information

...ngth: 140 miles, in a figure of eight ...m Harlow to Cambridge and back
...oing: easy
...S maps: 154, 166, 167

...he Way explores the quiet ...ssex and Cambridgeshire ...ountryside. From the busy ...iver Stort the path goes up ...nd down gentle hills and val...ys (there are good views ...bove Newport) to Saffron ...Walden and on past Bartlow ...umuli to Cambridge. The ...eturn is on ancient track...ays through Thaxted with its ...istoric windmill and 15th-...entury Guildhall.

...t Peter's Way

...ssential Information

...ngth: 45 miles, from Chipping Ongar ...Bradwell-on-Sea
...oing: easy
...S maps: 167, 168

...rewarding walk at all seasons, ...e Way is predominantly field ...nd track walking, with ...tretches of marshland and ...easide creeks. The route from ...Ongar is via Blackmore, Stock, ...here there is a windmill, ...Ianningfield Reservoir to ...urleigh, with views of the ...lackwater estuary, and finally ...) Bradwell.

...uggested Walking Areas

Great Dunmow

...splendid circular walk of ...1½ miles through Little ...aston Manor and Great ...aston.

Epping Forest.

● Great Waltham

An 8-mile circular walk through Fanner's Green, with distant views of Chelmsford.

● Harlow

A pleasant 4½-mile circular route from Old Harlow.

● Lea and Stort Valleys

There is a 5-mile circular walk from Roydon over field paths and along the escarpment, with views of the Lea Valley and the Stort at Roydon.

● North Weald

A 5-mile circular walk runs from North Weald to Ongar Park Hall.

● Roding Valley

A 5-mile circular route from Fyfield on the River Roding runs over green fields and tracks and along the river bank.

● Roxwell

This pretty 4½-mile circular walk takes in Patience Bridge, Roxwell Brook and Tye Hall.

● Stock

A 9½-mile circular walk from the village of Stock runs along tracks on high ground to Hanningfield Reservoir.

OS maps: 154, 167, 168, 169, 177

Greater London

The London Countryway (see pages 22-23) circles the capital and is within easy reach for day or weekend outings. Part of the Epping Forest Centenary Walk also runs through Greater London (see page 40-41).

The Canal Walk

Essential Information

Length: 26 miles, from Limehouse to Uxbridge, with an additional 5-mile link from Brentford Dock
Going: easy
OS maps: 176, 177

This is a unique walk from east to west through London. The areas passed may be familiar, but the view is totally different, recalling the canal's heyday in the early 19th century. The towpath starts at Salmon Lane Lock by Limehouse Basin, where the Regent's Canal flows into the Thames. Past the Mile End Road, the path runs alongside Victoria Park to Old Ford, where there is a charming, almost rural, group of canalside buildings. All along this stretch are old canal basins and fine warehouses. There is no towpath through Islington Tunnel, and walkers must go overground. Past St Pancras Basin, and the magnificent view of the station, the targets are Camden Town (5¾ miles) and Little Venice. Between the two, the walker skirts London Zoo, runs alongside Regent's Park and again must go overground at Maida Hill Tunnel. At Little Venice, where a number of houseboats are moored, the Canal joins the Paddington branch of the Grand Union Canal. Running under the Westway Flyover, the canal makes for Kensal Green, passes the huge cemetery, Willesden Junction (11½ miles) and the Park Royal Industrial Estate. The canal now runs through suburbia, with housing and factories developed in the first half of the present century. Sudbury golf course precedes Horsenden Hill, and then it is a short way to Ruislip and Bull's Bridge, where the Paddington branch meets the Grand Union Main Line from Brentford.

The link path from Brentford follows this Main Line, which

The Serpentine, Hyde Park.

Grand Union Canal, Little Venice.

runs down to the Thames at Brentford. The 5-mile walk is positively rural, going past Boston Manor Park to Hanwell Locks. This flight of six locks raises the canal 53 feet and takes a barge 90 minutes to clear. Then come Three Bridges, where road, rail and water meet, and finally Bull's Bridge.

The London Silver Jubilee Walkway

Essential Information

Length: 10 miles, starting and finishing at Leicester Square
Going: easy, but on pavements
OS map: 176

Created in 1977 to celebrate Queen Elizabeth II's Silver Jubilee, this path runs through the heart of London. Highlights of the route are: Parliament Square, the South Bank, Southwark Cathedral, Tower Hill, St Paul's Cathedral and the Barbican.

Suggested Walking Areas

● London's Parks

In both inner and outer London, the city's parks have a deservedly high reputation. An especially fine park walk in central London is from Notting Hill Gate to Parliament Square.

Enter Kensington Gardens at the north-west corner and strike across to the Serpentine and through Hyde Park to Hyde Park Corner. Having negotiated the complex subways, emerge into Green Park and then cross The Mall into St James's Park. Except for road crossings, this is an entirely green route.

Of the many parks and open spaces away from central London these are especially recommended:
Victoria Park, Hackney
Hampstead Heath
Dulwich Park
Wimbledon Common
On the fringe of London, there are plenty of open spaces, often merging into country 'proper'. Recommended circular walks are:

● Outer London (south)

Kingston to Hampton Court (5½ miles)
Eel Pie Island to Marble Hill and Richmond Park (6½ miles)
Roehampton, Wimbledon Common and Richmond Park (6½ miles)
Kenley to Old Coulsdon (7¾ miles)
Great Farleigh Green and Sanderstead (7½ miles)
Biggin Hill and Keston (8 miles)
Chislehurst and Petts Wood (6½ miles)

● Outer London (north)

Hendon Church End to Brent Bridge (6¼ miles)
Totteridge and Mill Hill (6¼ miles)
Stanmore to Elstree (8½ miles)
Kenton to Harrow-on-the-Hill (4 miles)
Cockfosters to Monken Hadley (7¼ miles)
Enfield to Cuffley (9 miles)

OS maps: 176, 177, 187

The West Country

There is a wealth of walking in these six westernmost counties, in wooded valleys, along the banks of rivers and streams and on hill-side paths, while in the background, a sense of the sea and a tang of adventure prevails. For those attracted by coastal paths, this corner of England offers some of the most spectacular cliff-top walking.

Exmoor, Dartmoor and the coastline: these are the highlights of the West Country. The South-West Peninsula Coast Path is Britain's longest long-distance path, over 500 miles. From Minehead in the north to Poole in the south it winds past secluded harbours and coves, along wind-swept cliffs and above crashing breakers. The two Moors each have their special characteristics: Exmoor, pleasantly rolling, with the bite of the sea in the air; Dartmoor, high and wild landscape with some uncompromisingly tough walking.

Here, then, are walks to suit all weathers, tastes and

1 Cornwall
2 Devon
3 Somerset
4 Avon
5 Wiltshire
6 Dorset

energies. Some sections of the South-West Peninsula Coast Path are definitely only for the dedicated enthusiast, but many more will be enjoyed by everyone. On the Moors, the climbs can be quite stiff, and map and compass, and a cautious eye on the weather, are needed. Elsewhere, though, the going is easy, the scenery gentle and inviting. From the beauty of the Mendip Hills to the wide skyline of the Salisbury Plain and the quintessential English country lanes of Hardy country in Dorset, the terrain could not be more varied.

Practical Points on Coastal Walking

● Knowledge of coastal walking comes with experience. Wet chalk can be very slippery and farmers sometimes fence dangerously close to cliff-tops edged by public paths.

● Gullies littered with shale and loose boulders should be crossed with care. Beware of the dangers of subsidence after prolonged wet weather.

● Remember the obvious danger of walking too close to cliff edges. Winds can gust fiercely across exposed headlands and over-growth may hide a cliff fissure.

● Coastal walking presents few navigational problems but do not dispense with large-scale maps or a compass.

● Routes can be strenuous, part-icularly for novice walkers, as paths follow natural contours. Take this into account when planning your daily mileage.

● Some coasts have good facilities for food and accommodation, but long distances may separate avail-able supplies on other stretches. Be prepared. Only backpackers enjoy total independence on long-distance coastal routes.

The South-West Peninsula Coast Path

Essential Information

Length: 510 miles, from Minehead (Somerset) to South Haven Point (Dorset)

Going: fairly easy for much of the way, but with occasional quite difficult sections and numerous ascents and descents

Terrain: coastline, rough and majestic on the Atlantic coast, softer on the Channel side

OS maps: 180, 181, 190, 192, 193, 194, 195, 200, 201, 202, 203, 204

This is the longest of Britain's long-distance paths, a challenging 510 miles around the entire south-west peninsula. Not many walkers will want to attempt the entire route – at least not all at once. But many stretches make an excellent week's or weekend's walk, and the potential for day expeditions is unlimited. Despite the crowds that regularly flock to the west country each summer, most of the Path is peaceful. And when a resort is encountered, its noise and bustle are soon left behind. The Path passes through the most varied and fascinating landscapes, and cliffs, sea-birds, wild flowers, and historic and legendary places all combine with the sheer majesty of the land to make an unforgettable walk.

Minehead to County Gate: 8 miles

The first short stretch lies in Somerset. From Minehead the walker climbs quite steeply up North Hill and over Selworthy Beacon. This is a good start to the walk and a taste of splendours to come. The Path descends to Selworthy and Porlock Weir, and then comes another climb up to the Devon border at County Gate, with views to Exmoor on the left and the sea on the right. On the way Culbone church is passed, said to be the smallest in England.

County Gate to Ilfracombe: 25 miles

After a short road section, there is a fine walk across Countis-

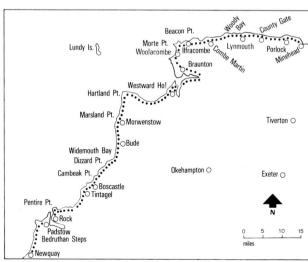

The Castle remains at Tintagel.

bury Common and down into Lynmouth. Now there is another ascent, over Hollerday Hill, followed by the dramatic Valley of the Rocks, then Woody Bay, Martinhoe Beacon, the Hunter's Inn, Trentishoe Down and Holdstone Down and finally an easy descent into Combe Martin. A relatively easy 6-mile stretch past Hele and around Beacon Point brings the walker into Ilfracombe.

Ilfracombe to Westward Ho!: 34 miles

This part of the route passes excellent surfing beaches, though there are more to come in Cornwall. Climbing out of the town towards Torrs Point, the walker makes first for Morte Point, then for Woolacombe and Croyde. The path turns inland to Braunton, where there is the first of several breaks in the Path. To regain the coast at Westward Ho! it is

necessary to go through Barnstaple and Bideford, although the summer ferry from Instow to Appledore cuts out the second of these two towns.

Westward Ho! to Bude: 34 miles

The first objective is Hartland Point, around which there is some fairly tough going. Now the landscape begins to change, becoming harsher and more rugged as the walker makes for Marsland Point and, over the Cornish border, Marsland Cliff and Bude, a pleasant resort and haunt of surfers. A detour inland to Morwenstow, where Robert Hawker, the village vicar and a celebrated poet, built a house of wrecked ships, is well worthwhile.

Bude to Padstow: 39 miles

This is the Cornwall of myth and legend. It takes little imagination to picture the wreckers waiting on the cliffs, the sea foaming below, the seagulls cawing in the wind. An easy stretch out of Bude to

47

THE SOUTH-WEST PENINSULA COAST PATH

Widemouth Sands may beguile the walker. But then there are hauls up Dizzard Point and on to Cambeak Point, Pentargon Cove and Boscastle, followed by one of the highlights of the entire 500 miles – the marvellous cliff walk to Tintagel. Leaving the majestic castle behind (its connections with King Arthur are spurious) the walker strides out round Dennis Point towards Port Isaac. After Pentire Point there is a stretch of beach-walking near Polzeath, almost an anticlimax, and then the ferry from Rock to Padstow.

Padstow to Perranporth: 28 miles

The walk to Newquay is relatively easy in comparison with what has gone before. But there are some spectacular cliffs, in particular Bedruthan Steps. Legend has it that these were the giant Bedruthan's stepping-stones. To regain solitude after the crowds in Newquay, take the ferry across the Gannel, or walk over the footbridge, and follow the Path through sand dunes to St Piran's church on Penhale Sands and then along Perran Beach to Perranporth.

Perranporth to Land's End: 50 miles

The final section on the Atlantic coast starts with a grand walk round St Agnes Head, past Hell's Mouth and round Godrevy Point. The walk into St Ives through Hayle and Carbis Bay is less interesting. But there is compensation ahead, an

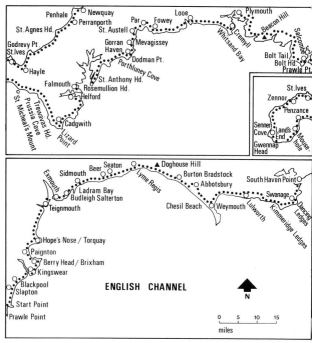

ENGLISH CHANNEL

N

0   5   10   15
miles

solated path along rough coastline. Once or twice the Path is hard to follow, and deviations inland, especially at Zennor and Morvah, are advisable. Finally, Whitesand Bay and Sennen Cove bring the walker to Land's End, the natural halfway mark of the coastal path.

Land's End to Porthleven: 83 miles

In fact, there are nearly 300 miles to come, and so the walker must leave this most romantic spot behind and stride out along the cliffs towards Mousehole, past Gwennap Head, Porthgwarra Cove, St Leven and the Minack Cliff Theatre. The coast is noticeably mellower here, the sea usually calmer, and secluded coves and fishing villages, now often the home of artists, succeed one another. There is a break in

above: Land's End.

below: Cliffs along the coast from Tintagel.

the Path at Penzance, and the walk resumes east of the town, making past St Michael's Mount for Prussia Cove, Par Sands and the climb to Trewavas Head.

49

THE WEST COUNTRY

THE SOUTH-WEST PENINSULA COAST PATH

Porthleven to Falmouth: 37 miles

This part of the Path takes the walker down the western side of the Lizard peninsula, round the point and up the eastern edge. It is a fine walk, with majestic cliffs and the occasional almost hidden cove. Highlights are the amazing rock formations at Kynance, Cadgwith and Carleon Cove. There are occasional inland stretches, usually to avoid quarries, and at Helford the river has to be crossed by ferry to complete the last stretch round Rosemullion Head and Pennance Point to Falmouth.

Falmouth to Par Sands: 33 miles

More ferries, this time across the estuary to St Anthony in Roseland, precede some fairly tough walking towards Porthluney Cove and even tougher terrain around Dodman Point. After Gorran Haven comes a popular stretch of coast, crowded in summer, around Mevagissey and Pentewan Sands. Near St Austell is both industry and tourism, although the china clay works do not encroach on the Path itself.

Par Sands to Cremyll: 39 miles

The next objectives are Polperro and Looe, with some fine walking to get there. Between the two, spend a little time in Fowey and Polruan, on opposite sides of the estuary of the River Fowey. They are enchanting towns, among Cornwall's best. The final Cornish stretch passes Whitsand Bay and descends towards the Tamar and the ferry over to Plymouth from Cremyll.

Plymouth to Dartmouth: 46 miles

Leaving Cornwall behind, the walker tackles Beacon Hill and then, after a short inland stretch, the marvellous route between Bolt Tail and Bolt Head and an enchanting climb down to Salcombe. Yet another ferry leads to yet another fine walk, this one round Prawle and Start Points. There is easy walking along Slapton Sand and Blackpool Sands, round Blackstone Point and into Dartmouth.

Dartmouth to Exmouth: 29 miles

The Path from Kingswear, across the Dart from Dartmouth, to Brixham is a pleasant walk, but rather disappointing if some of the preceding sections have been tackled. Then comes the Torbay conurbation. There are plenty of attractions here, but good walking is not among them. On the eastern side, ferries to Teignmouth and then across the Exe to Exmouth follow in short succession.

Exmouth to Lyme Regis: 29 miles

Proper walking can resume now unhampered by resorts and crowds. Budleigh Salterton, Ladram Bay and Peak Hill bring the walker to Sidmouth, and then there is a pleasant cliff-top walk to Branscombe and on to Beer and Seaton. Then, after the golf course, comes a tricky approach to Lyme Regis through the celebrated landslip, where the Path is indistinct and often fairly hard going. But the town is worth the effort, especially for Jane Austen and John Fowles enthusiasts.

Dancing Ledge, near Swanage, a rock formation of Portland Stone.

Lyme Regis to Weymouth: 35 miles

The Peninsula Path runs through four counties, and Dorset is the last. But there is still a way to go, and in many respects the walking is tougher here, with plenty of switchback ascents and descents, than in Devon, which seems soft and mild in comparison. Leaving Lyme Regis, Timber Hill and Doghouse Hill have to be tackled. But then comes one of the most interesting and unusual walks of the entire Path. Past Burton Bradstock the Path keeps to sea level through West Boxington and inland to Abbotsbury, home of the famous swannery. Then it returns to the sea and runs along Chesil Beach, the 10-mile long pebble bank swept up by the tides, and into Weymouth.

An alternative route strikes inland three miles east of Burton Bradstock, climbs high behind Weymouth and returns to the coast east of the town at Osmington Mills. This is a fine and exhilarating walk, but a map is essential, since this section of the Path is not always clearly defined.

Weymouth to South Haven Point: 37 miles

Black Head, White Nothe, Bat's Head and Durdle Door are all landmarks on the way to Lulworth, a brisk walk with plenty of ups and downs. After Lulworth a detour inland may be necessary if the army firing-ranges are in operation, but in any case the coast is clear after Worbarrow. Past Kimmeridge are some of the highlights of the walk: Kimmeridge Ledges, St Alban's Head, Chapman's Pool, Dancing Ledge, Tilly Whim Caves and Great Globe. The seabirds whirl, the waves crash on rocks beneath, and the walker catches a wonderful sense of exhilaration. After Swanage the Path concludes with a simple stretch over the Purbeck Hills and along Studland Bay to South Haven Point.

Cornwall

The South-West Peninsula Coast Path (see pages 46-51) follows the entire Cornish coast, from Marsland Mouth in the north to Cremyll in the south.

Suggested Walking Areas

● Bodmin Moor

There are 12 square miles of moorland and good walking, with ascents to Brown Willy (at 1,375 feet the highest point in the county) and Rough Tor (1,311 feet). The walk up Brown Willy from the 18th-century Jamaica Inn, made famous by Daphne du Maurier's novel, is especially fine. Always take a compass on Bodmin Moor, as the mists can roll down in minutes and deprive the most experienced walker of a sense of direction.

● Cadgwith

A pretty 3-mile nature trail begins at Ruan Minor near Cadgwith and passes waterfalls, cliffs and caves.

● Cardinham Woods

Two miles east of Bodmin are four trails, 1½ to 3 miles long, through a steep wooded valley.

Brown Willy seen from Rough Tor.

● St Cleer

This village is the start of a good 3-mile walk on the edge of Bodmin Moor up to King Doniert's Stone (he was a famous Cornish king) and on to Trevethey Stone and up Caradon Hill, 1,212 feet.

● Deerpark

The Deerpark Forest Trail starts at the picnic site on the Herodsfoot road off the B3359 Looe road and runs through a typical Cornish wooded valley with interesting wildlife.

● Halvana

Two miles on the Tregirls road from Five Lanes Village on the A30 is the start of a fascinating 1½-mile trail through spruce and pine woods and past historical and industrial sites.

● Llanhydrock

A 2-mile nature trail runs through woods and along the River Fowey from the National Trust signpost 2 miles south of Bodmin off the B3268.

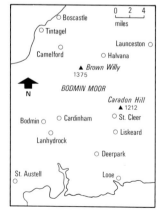

OS maps: 190, 200, 201, 203, 204

Devon

The South-West Peninsula Coast Path runs the length of both Devon's coastlines, south and north (see pages 46-51). There are many fine and exhilarating walks. In particular, in the north, from the Somerset border at County Gate to Lynmouth, into Combe Martin and Westward Ho! round Hartland Point to Marsland Mouth. In the south the walks of note are Thurlestone to Salcombe around Bolt Tail and Bolt Head and on to Torcross Prawle and Start Points.

Two Moors Way

Essential Information

Length: 101 miles, from Ivybridge to Lynmouth

Going: varied, with some easy stretches and some quite hard patches over high ground

OS maps: 180, 181, 191, 202

The Way runs from south to north across Devon, linking Dartmoor and Exmoor. It is a rugged walk. The land is hilly and can be wet and unwelcoming; protective clothing and map and compass are essential.

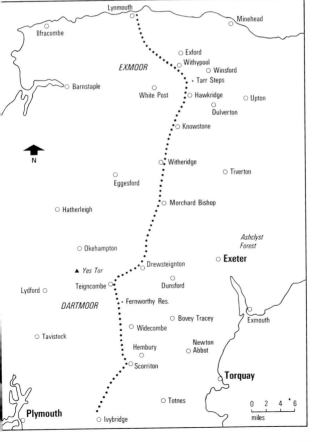

THE WEST COUNTRY

DEVON

The massive granite Hound Tor, on Dartmoor, from where Haytor Rocks can be seen.

Ivybridge to Teigncombe: 31 miles

The walker starts at the deep end, with a long stretch across Dartmoor to Scorriton. This is open, hostile land, with remains of Bronze Age settlements to be seen by the path, and evidence of tin and china clay workings too. After Scorriton there is a series of hills before the B3357 Princetown to Ashburton road is crossed. After more moorland walking a short stretch on the Mariners' Way is reached. This is an old track from Bideford to Dartmouth, said to have been used by sailors.

Teigncombe to Hawkridge: 44 miles

The Way follows the Teign Valley (a higher alternative route passes near Castle Drogo) to Drewsteignton and shortly afterwards leaves the Dartmoor National Park. There is a true change of scenery here, wild moorland giving way to rich, gently rolling agricultural land. Morchard Bishop, Witheridge and Knowstone succeed one another, and just north of West Anstey the walker crosses into the Exmoor National Park.

Hawkridge to Lynmouth: 26 miles

The Way to Withypool follows the lovely Barle Valley past Tarr Steps, although after wet weather a diversion on higher ground, over Parsonage Down and Withypool Hill, may be necessary. After Withypool it is high level walking again across lonely land, with views of the Bristol Channel. The last stretch from Hoar Oak has a spectacular climax, following a path along the Cleaves above the East Lyn River and then descending sharply into Lynmouth.

Suggested Walking Areas

● Ashclyst

Several forest walks run through Ashclyst Forest south of the B3181 near Exeter.

● Bovey Tracey

The Yarner Wood nature trail runs for 3¼ miles through pleasant woodland and past old industrial sites.

● Dartmoor

Dartmoor deserves a word of caution. Walkers should stick to the paths, which are well beaten, and should not venture far without map and compass. The weather is changeable and can easily turn treacherous quickly and quite unexpectedly. Recommended walks on the Moor include:
Cadover Bridge to Trowlesworthy Warren (2 miles)
Postbridge to Fernworthy Reservoir (5 miles)
Buckfastleigh to Princetown along the Abbots' Way
Widecombe in the Moor to Haytor Rocks
Postbridge to Bellever Forest and Tor (3 miles)

● Dunsford

A 4-mile nature trail runs through the Dunsford Nature Reserve on the banks of the Teign.

● Eggesford

The Heywood Forest Walk is a 2½-miles route through Flashdown Woods near Eggesford. There are good views from this Douglas fir plantation.

● Exmoor

This is a pleasanter walking area, the walking high and isolated yet not quite so challenging. Most of the National Park lies in Somerset (for walks there see pages 56-57). Recommended walks in the Devon part are:
Lynbridge to Watersmeet circular (6 miles)
East Anstey to Tarr Steps (5 miles)
Combe Martin to Hunters Inn circular (13 miles)
Hunters Inn to Heddon's Mouth along the Heddon Valley (4 miles)

● Fernworthy

A 1½-mile forest trail gives wide views of Dartmoor and the reservoir.

● Hatherleigh

There is a fine 3-mile walk along the banks of the River Lew and Medland Brook south of the town.

● Hembury Woods

These fine oak woods south of Ashburton have a fine 1½-mile forest walk.

● Loddiswell

There are 2 miles of footpaths on the east bank of the River Avon near Kingsbridge.

● Lydford

Lydford Woods offer an attractive 2-mile forest trail.

OS maps: 180, 181, 190, 191, 192, 193, 201, 202

Somerset

The start of the 510-mile South-West Peninsula Coast Path is in Somerset (see page 46).

The West Mendip Way

Essential Information

Length: 30 miles, from Wells to Uphill, Weston-super-Mare (Avon)
Going: easy, but with some climbs
OS map: 182

This is a hill path along the ridge of the Mendips from the magnificent cathedral city of Wells to the popular seaside delights of Weston-super-Mare. From Wells the first targets are Arthur's Point and Wookey Hole, where early Britons dwelt in the caves. After Ebbor there is high open terrain to Priddy, home of the Mendip Sheep Fair, and more upland walking until the descent to Cheddar. Next comes Rowberrow Warren (once part of the royal forest of Mendip), Shipham, Winterhead Hill and Crook Peak. After Loxton the final stretch is up Bleadon and Purn Hills and down to Uphill, a couple of miles along the beach from Weston town centre.

Suggested Walking Areas

● Brendon Hills

These hills are a pleasant cultivated area slightly to the east of Exmoor proper. Recommended walks are:
Wheddon Cross to Lype Hill via Putham Ford (2¾ miles)
Brompton Regis to Kennisham Wood (3½ miles)
Clatworthy to Raleighs Cross (2½ miles)
Pitt Farm to Brendon Hill (5½ miles)
Kingsbridge to Treborough (2¾ miles)

● Broadway

The Castle Neroche Forest Walks are two trails, 1½ and 2½ miles long, starting 3 miles west of Broadway on a minor road off the A303.

● Cheddar Gorge

Fine walks here include:
Longwood Nature Trail, a lovely wooded 2½-mile walk starting above the upper end of the gorge.
Black Rock Nature Trail, 2 miles from the upper end of the gorge. The 2½-mile **Gorge Path**

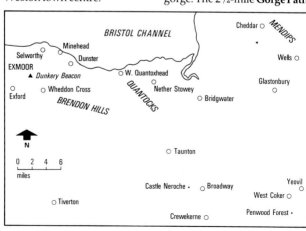

climbs up Jacob's Ladder and runs on to Black Rock Gate.

● **Dunster**

This is a delightful village, and a good walking centre. Nearby walks are:
Dunster to Withycombe (2¾ miles)
Dunster to Luxborough (5 miles)

● **Exmoor**

Exmoor falls partly in Somerset, partly in Devon. (For walks in the Devon section see page 55).

There are many fascinating footpaths, including:
Malmsmead and the Doone Valley (4½ miles)
Stoke Pero to Dunkery Beacon (2 miles), just one of the many ascents of the Beacon
Oare to Exford via Alderman's Barrow (8½ miles), a true Exmoor walk for which map and compass are essential
Exford to Winsford (5½ miles) via the Exe Valley
Simonsbath to Landacre on the valley route (5¼ miles) and over high ground (5 miles)

● **Exmoor Walks**

Dulverton to Tarr Steps and Withypool (9½ miles), one of the best on Exmoor
Dulverton to Winsford (5½ miles) across stimulating high land
Exford to Winsford Hill (3 miles)
White Post to Withypool (3½ miles)
Hartford to Upton (3 miles) along a broad track known as Lady Acland's Drive

● **Minehead**

North Hill and Selworthy Beacon above the town have a fascinating network of paths.

Blagdon Lake and the Mendip Hills.

Two recommended routes take in most of the area:
Minehead to Bossington Hill and Bossington Beach (5 miles)
Minehead Higher Town to Selworthy (3½ miles)

● **Nether Stowey**

At the foot of the Quantocks the Seven Wells Forest Trail runs for 2 miles from Nether Stowey.

● **Quantock Hills**

A fine striding ridge path runs for 7 miles along the centre of the Quantocks from West Quantoxhead to Birches Corner. A network of smaller paths criss-crosses the Hills.

● **Wells**

The 3-mile Wells Trail runs through fields and woodlands on the eastern side of the city.

● **West Coker**

At Penwood Forest there is a 2-mile forest trail, quite steep in places. A badger sett and a wildlife conservation pond are passed.

● **Wookey**

The 4-mile Moors Trail runs between Easton Church and Wookey.

OS maps: 172, 180, 181, 182, 183, 193, 194

Avon

The Cotswold Way (see page 70) and the West Mendip Way (see page 56) both run through Avon.

But the Kennet and Avon Canal can be followed through Wiltshire and Berkshire towards London (see pages 60 and 34).

The Avon Walkway

Essential Information

Length: 27½ miles, from Pill to Dundas Aqueduct
Going: easy
OS map: 172

Frome Valley Walkway

Essential Information

Length: 6 miles, from Frenchay to Iron Acton
Going: easy
OS map: 173

The Avon Walkway runs along the banks of the River Avon from Pill, a little way short of the junction with the Bristol Channel, right through the centre of Bristol and on eastwards to Bath and the Dundas Aqueduct on the Kennet and Avon Canal. There is some field walking to begin with through Paradise Bottom and Nightingale Valley. The first landmark is Brunel's dramatic suspension bridge over the gorge at Clifton. Then comes a fascinating section through the Bristol docks, past the *S.S. Great Britain*. The path here sticks to the river rather than the feeder canal built to bring water to the docks. Beyond St Anne's Weir at Netham the targets are Hanham Lock, Keynsham, the Georgian splendours of Bath, and finally Dundas Aqueduct, the official end of the Walkway.

This is an interesting and attractive walk along the banks of the fast-flowing River Frome. The route begins at Frenchay Lower Mill, continues to Cleeve Bridge where a short detour can be made to Cleeve Mills, originally a grist mill and one of the best preserved of the many mills along the river. Other features along the path are the pound at Hambrook, once used to keep stray animals, Bury Hill Camp, a Celtic and later a Roman settlement, Winterbourne Viaduct (built at the turn of the century), the 19th-century hat factory at Watley's End and Roden Acre mine. The tramway that carried the iron ore to the railway at Iron Acton can still be seen here. The end of the walk is at the curiously named Chill Wood, where depressions mark the position of a 17th-century coal mine.

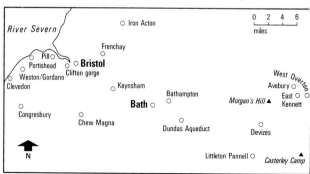

The Suspension Bridge at Clifton spans the Avon Gorge.

Suggested Walking Areas

● Avon Gorge

A series of forest walks begins at Leigh Woods off the A369 Bristol to Portishead road.

● Bristol Channel

A coastal path runs between Portishead and Clevedon, offering good views of the Channel and the frequent shipping.

● Brockley Combe

Three miles north-west of Congresbury a nature trail runs through the woods and the limestone gorge.

● Chew Magna

There is a good walk round Chew Valley Lake (famed for its trout fishing) starting from the village, which has a fine 15th-century bridge.

● Frenchay

The Frome Valley Nature Trail runs for 2¾ miles along the River Frome from Eastville Park to Frenchay Bridge and the Lower Mill, starting-point of the Frome Valley Walkway.

● Gordano Valley and Weston Moor Nature Reserve

There is a 10-mile walk round this attractive valley, situated between Clevedon and Clapton-in-Gordano, with additional footpaths for shorter expeditions. The natural life here is fascinating, and Weston Big Wood is a good example of semi-natural woodland.

● Kennet and Avon Canal

A 2-mile nature trail leads along the towpath from Widcombe to Bathampton.

● River Severn

There is a pleasant path between Oldbury and Shepperdine along the east bank of the Severn.

OS maps: 162, 172, 173, 182, 183

Wiltshire

The westernmost section of the Ridgeway Path (see pages 20-21) runs through the county.

Silbury Hill from the east.

Suggested Walking Areas

● Avebury

An interesting path leads from Overton Hill to West Kennet and the long barrow, the largest Neolithic chambered tomb in England, and then over Silbury Hill, the largest prehistoric mound in western Europe. Nearby, off the A361, another path climbs Windmill Hill, where a Neolithic settlement was formed in about 3700BC.

● Kennet & Avon Canal

There are good towpath walks all along the canal as it crosses Wiltshire. The staircase of 29 locks west of Devizes is especially interesting.

● Old Sarum

A pleasant 4½-mile walk leads from Salisbury to Old Sarum, the original site of Salisbury, and a 'rotten borough' until parliamentary reform in 1832.

● Salisbury Plain

The Ridgeway continues south-west from East Kennett, where the long-distance path starts, towards the coast. A good stretch along Salisbury Plain is between Casterley Camp, south-west of Upavington, and the A360 south o Littleton Pannell.

● Savernake Forest

There are many pleasant walks in this 2,500-acre forest, much of which was created in the 18th century by Capability Brown. The Grand Avenue, a 3-mile avenue of beeches, makes a marvellous walk, and other routes leave Eight Walks, a junction halfway along the Grand Avenue.

● Wansdyke

This ancient ditch originally ran from east of Marlborough to the Bristol Channel. A well-preserved stretch leads from the White Horse south of West Overton west across the A361 to Morgan's Hill.

● West Harnham

The old Exeter road, now long since replaced by the modern A30, took the ridge route from Salisbury to Shaftesbury. There is an excellent 13-mile stretch of green lane from West Harnham, just outside Salisbury, to White Sheet Hill, near Shaftesbury, the only hilltop town in Dorset.

OS maps: 163, 172, 173, 174, 183, 184, 195

Dorset

The South-West Peninsula Coast Path (see pages 46-51) follows Dorset's coastline. There is dramatic walking, especially from Kimmeridge to St Alban's Head and on to Swanage, and along Chesil Beach.

Suggested Walking Areas

● Bridport

There is a fine circular walk from Bridport through the Brit Valley to Beaminster and back. Leave the town via Pymore Mills and follow the east bank of the Brit to Netherbury and Beaminster, a lively market town with a fine church and almshouses. A delightful walk across Coombe Down Hill leads to Mapperton, past the posy tree, reputed to be the place where survivors of bubonic plague gathered to pray and collect protective herbs. The return is via Stoke Abbot or, a slightly shorter route, through Broadwindsor.

● Cerne Abbas

From Cerne Abbas village footpaths lead uphill past the ruined abbey to the 'Giant', 180 feet high. He is thought to date from the 2nd century AD and to represent the God Hercules. Later he became a fertility symbol, for obvious reasons, and May Day festivities took place on the hillside.

● Dorchester

This 3-mile walk commemorates the novelist Thomas Hardy, one of Dorset's most famous sons. Lower Bockhampton, where Hardy went to school, is the first objective, followed by Higher Bockhampton and Puddletown Heath, where Hardy was born. Then walk through Kingston Park to Stinsford Church, where the novelist's first wife is buried, and on to West Stafford.

● Higher Bockhampton

The 1½-mile Thorncombe Trail is a pleasant walk through mixed woodland.

● Maiden Newton

There is a 9-mile walk from Maiden Newton to Bridport along the track of the disused Bridport Railway, opened in 1857 and closed in 1975. The line runs along the Hooke Valley, near Toller Fratrum, an outpost of Forde Abbey, through Toller Porcorum and Witherstone Cutting and through the Powerstock Common Nature Reserve.

● Puddletown

From Beacon Corner, 1 mile from Puddletown, the Puddletown Forest Trail is a pleasant walk through woodland to a viewpoint overlooking the forest and the Purbeck Hills.

● Wootton Hill

The Forest Trail here is 1¼ miles long, and runs through a semi-mature plantation of mixed trees. The start is 3 miles north of Lyme Regis, off the Wootton Fitzpaine road from the A35.

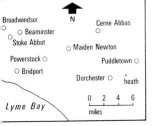

OS maps: 183, 184, 193, 194, 195

Wales and The Borders

Wales and the border lands have the reputation of mountain country. Snowdon and Cader Idris are the celebrated peaks, and there are also the Brecon Beacons, the Presely Hills and the Black Mountains. Although the Welsh uplands can prove dangerous if under-estimated, slightly easier routes for walkers have been selected here. Occasionally a little scrambling may be required – but no more than that. And at the summits, spectacular views and long plateau walks await, the land rolling out in front as the walker strides out.

Elsewhere the going is easier but no less enjoyable: the rolling hills of the Marches – Malverns, Stiperstones, Wenlock Edge; exhilarating paths above the industrial valleys of South Wales; routes past ancient settlements and, like Glyndwr's Way, near places celebrated in Welsh history. And then there is the coast: gentle in the north

1   Gloucestershire
2   Hereford and Worcester
3   Shropshire
4   Clwyd
5   Gwynedd
6   Powys
7   Dyfed
8   West Glamorgan
9   Mid Glamorgan
10 South Glamorgan
11 Gwent

more rugged in the south, on the Gower Peninsula and in Dyfed.

There are two long-distance paths. The Pembrokeshire Coast Path runs from east of Tenby along a spectacular coastline west and then north to Cardigan. The walk is well worthwhile, with some quite tough isolated sections and many more that are exhilarating but not unduly difficult. The same pattern applies to Offa's Dyke Path, which crisscrosses the English/Welsh border. Some map and compass work is required on the high parts, which more than repay the climb, and there are plenty of lower-lying stretches.

Practical Points on Hill Walking

● Never underestimate hill contours. Even the most compact group of hills will take a toll from under-used leg muscles.

● To conserve energy keep to the same contour line where possible. This applies particularly when distance-walking in wilder hills.

● It is often almost as tiring on muscles to descend as to ascend, especially towards the end of an energetic day. Do not hurry the descent or front thigh muscles may tighten, which will incapacitate you for the next day.

● While navigation is not quite so vital on southern hills, in the North, Wales, and Scotland constant reference to map and compass may be needed.

● Make sure that at least one member of the party is properly proficient with map and compass.

● On any two-day expedition, or longer, try to select an overnight location on high ground if possible. Metabolism is low early in the morning, and that is no time to face a stiff climb back to the tops.

● Do not overload your rucksack, whatever the temptation.

Offa's Dyke Path

Essential Information

Length: 168 miles, from Sedbury Cliffs, on the banks of the Severn, to Prestatyn
Going: some relatively gentle walking, but generally hard – sometimes very hard
Terrain: chiefly high ground, windy and cold, especially in winter, with frequent ups and downs; some valley walking
OS maps: 16, 117, 126, 137, 148, 161, 162

This Path commemorates Offa, king of Mercia from 757 to 796.

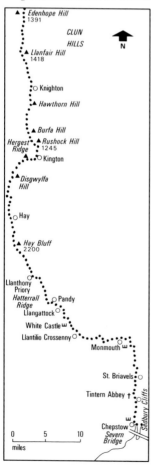

The Dyke was built towards the end of his reign, to mark the border with Wales. Today some 81 miles remain clearly defined, and the long-distance path follows the original route whenever practicable, criss-crossing the Welsh/English border from the Severn estuary in the south to the seaside resort of Prestatyn in the north. There is much of historical interest along the Path, the scenery could not be more varied, and the conditions are challenging for much of the way. Except in the gentlest sections, some walking experience is necessary, and map and compass should be carried.

Chepstow to Pandy (32 miles)

Strictly speaking, Sedbury Cliffs are the start of the Path, but Chepstow is the best place to begin. The medieval streets run up to the 13th-century castle, perched high above the river Wye.

Following a path from the town centre, the Way runs past Tutshill and along the fringe of the Forest of Dean, with the Wye below. The Forest, once a royal hunting ground, covers 50 square miles. The highlight of this first stretch is the view of the 13th-century Tintern Abbey from the Devil's Pulpit; the climb down to the ruins can be hard and slippery. There are two routes to St Briavels: along the towpath or on the hills, tracing the line of the Dyke. The next objective is Monmouth, where shopping can be done and the 17th-century castle and the Nelson Museum visited.

The 16 miles to Pandy are easier going, though still tough in places, through Llantilio-Crossenny and White Castle,

above: The Forest of Dean.
below: Chepstow Castle.

which commands fine views. Now there are fields and a river crossing before Llangattock, where the celebrated buccaneer Captain Morgan, governor of Jamaica, is buried. Within a mile or so the majestic Hatterrall Ridge looms into view, promise of hard walking ahead. But first there is Pandy, a good place for a rest.

Pandy to Kington (32 miles)

The 17 miles to Hay-on-Wye should only be tackled in good weather: the Path is high, desolate in places, and the weather can turn all too quickly. But the Ridge is marvellous, the only sign of life the birds and the Welsh cobs and ponies that use the hills for grazing. The Path descends to the lovely Llanthony Priory, a 12th-century ruin in a picturesque

65

meadowed valley. The route runs north now across a dark peat plateau, the going hard to Hay Bluff, where the views of Radnor Forest and the Silurian Hills are impressive. The drop down to Hay, a pretty market town whose bookshops make a browser's paradise, is relatively easy. The next section is greener, and there is open walking on Disgwylfa Hill and Hergest Ridge before another descent to Kington.

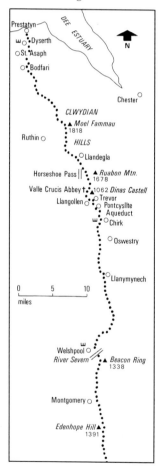

Kington to Montgomery (34 miles)

The first stage, to Knighton, halfway along the Path and headquarters of the Offa's Dyke Association, can be quite hard going. Rushock Hill follows Bradnor Hill, then there is a drop to the Vale of Radnor, and a climb again, to Burfa Hill. The views in all directions are superb.

After Knighton the Clun Hills present challenging ridge walking. Llanfair Hill is the highest point of the Path. The Dyke here is clearly visible, especially on Edenhope Hill and again on the stretch running to Montgomery.

Montgomery to Trevor (29 miles)

The next stretch has some road-walking, and if there has been rain the going can be heavy. There is a long climb to Beacon Hill, and then the Path falls to cross the Severn. A detour to Welshpool is worthwhile, especially to the fascinating 16th-century castle, situated in a vast park. Further on, beyond Llanymynech, there is quite hard walking past Oswestry and Chirk. Above Nanteris there is a good section of Dyke, the last the walker will see, and then woodland paths and roads run into Trevor. An alternative route crosses the celebrated Pontcysyllte aqueduct: not for vertigo-sufferers, it stretches 1,000 feet across the River Dee, 120 feet above the tumbling waters.

Trevor to Prestatyn (41 miles)

After Trevor there is wild country on the Panorama walk, and past ruined Dinas Castle to

The hills above Llangollen.

Llangollen, where a diversion along the canal to the ruins of the 13th-century Valle Crucis Abbey is a must. The Path itself runs through the huge Horseshoe Pass and the gentle Eglwyseg valley before climbing to the moors. After Llandegla there is a hard stretch across the Clwydian Hills, past Iron Age hill-forts. The miles on to Bodfari present challenge after challenge, with fine views the reward at each summit. At Moel Fammau the hills reach 1,820 feet, with views across to Cader Idris and Snowdon.

The last section is almost an anti-climax, 10 miles of easier going through woods and along roads through St Asaph and past Dyserth Castle to the final panorama above Prestatyn and the conclusion of one of the country's most challenging paths.

67

The Pembrokeshire Coast Path

Essential Information

Length: 168 miles, from Amroth near
Tenby to St Dogmaels, Cardigan
Going: generally fairly tough, with
some easy stretches and some very
difficult ones
Terrain: chiefly coastal, with numerous
ascents and descents; a few inland
stretches
OS Maps: 145, 157, 158

This path is a majestic coast
walk from Amroth on the
shores of Carmarthen Bay in
the south to St Dogmaels, just
outside Cardigan, in the north.
The going is tough in parts and
the country isolated.

Amroth to Tenby: 6 miles

The Path starts vigorously,
with a stiff climb up from
Amroth and then quite rough
cliff-top walking. At Saunders-
foot the way follows a 19th-
century tunnel through an
anthracite mine. Further on towards Tenby, there are fine sea
views.

Tenby to Freshwater West: 28 miles

From Tenby the first goal is
Manorbier Castle, which long
pre-dates the Normans who
extended and strengthened it.
This is quite an easy stretch,
with an alternative route
around Giltar Point. Beyond
Manorbier, it is more easy walking to the sands at Freshwater
East, then invigorating cliff
tops around Stackpole Quay
and Head. There is Ministry of
Defence land at St Govan's
Head and an inland diversion
may be necessary if warning
flags are flying. If possible continue along the coast to Stack
Rocks. Then the Path turns
inland, regaining the coast at
Freshwater West.

Wooltack Point seen from Marloes Peninsula.

Freshwater West to Pembroke: 18 miles

Stamina is needed for the Path around the headland, but there is an easier alternative along lanes a little way inland. Angle village precedes a gentler walk, with views across to Milford Haven, through Lambeeth, past Monkton Priory and into Pembroke.

Pembroke to Marloes: 30 miles

The walk is best resumed beyond Milford Haven: the town's large oil refineries may be impressive structures, but they do not make for good walking. The causeway at Sandy Haven can only be crossed at low tide. Then there is woodland, rock cliffs and mud flats before Dale is reached. There is a short cut straight across the headland to Westdale Bay and Marloes, but that means missing St Ann's Head, where the sea pounds on the rocks.

Marloes to Porth-clais: 31 miles

It is a remote walk from Marloes around Wooltack Point, where there are good views of Skomer and Skokholm islands, both nature reserves. Then the Path becomes easier, eventually reaching a fine beach between Broad Haven and Newgale. Before Solva the Path is a switchback but easy to follow. Once the pretty harbour is left behind, there is an overgrown stretch, but from Caerfai the going is easy. St David's with its magnificent cathedral is an essential detour here.

Porth-clais to Fishguard: 30 miles

The Path around the headland to Whitesand Bay and on up the coast to Porth-gain is easy, with splendid views and a series of ancient forts and burial mounds. But the next stretch, round Strumble Head, is not for the inexperienced, who should take the easier paths inland. The coastal walk is an exciting challenge: rough, often slippery, with seabirds and crashing waves the only companions. Well past the point the Path begins to descend, and the last few miles into Fishguard are relatively easy in comparison with what has already been achieved.

Fishguard to St Dogmaels: 25 miles

The Path to Newport is the best kind of walking: open, with lovely views and a real sense of space. There is a short cut which misses out Dinas Head, but the longer alternative is well worth the effort. The last 13 miles are a fitting climax. The going is hard but not impossible, and the Path clear, with majestic cliffs and crags. Past Cemaes Head it drops to Poppit Sands and St Dogmaels, just a short walk from Cardigan.

Gloucestershire

Offa's Dyke Path (see pages 64-67) touches the fringes of the county, as does the Oxfordshire Way (see page 35).

The Cotswold Way

Essential Information

Length: 95 miles, from Chipping Campden to Bath (Avon)
Going: mostly easy
OS maps: 151, 162, 163, 172

This magnificent path runs virtually the entire length of the Cotswold Hills. The start is at Chipping Campden, almost the quintessential Cotswold town, the stone of the houses glowing mellow. Chipping Campden was made prosperous by the wool trade, and the Woolstaplers Hall Museum is worth a visit. Making for Broadway, the Way runs along The Mile Drive and over an ancient trackway known as Buckle Street. There are consistently good views, among them Stanton from Shenberrow Hill. Before Winchcombe, the Way passes the ruins of Hailes Abbey, founded in the 13th century. Next come Sudeley Castle and Cleeve Common, at 1,083 feet the highest point in the Cotswolds. There is a stretch of lowland walking now, past Seven Springs, before high ground again at Ravensgate and Wistley Hills. After the Devil's Chimney on Leckhampton Hill, the walker comes to Cooper's Hill (43 miles), where the annual cheese-rolling ceremony takes place. Painswick Beacon and Painswick itself are quickly passed, before the railway, the Stroudwater Canal and the River Frome are crossed in rapid succession. Then it is along Stanley Wood, past Uleybury Fort into Dursley, where there is an impressive 18th-century Market House. Wotton-under-Edge is the next town, then the villages of Little Sodbury, Tormarton and Pennsylvania. The final stretch runs over Sion Hill and finally down to the splendours of Bath.

Suggested Walking Areas

● Cheltenham

The hills around Cheltenham offer excellent walking possibilities:
Leckhampton to Pegglesworth and Charlton Kings (11 miles)
Shurdington to Crickley Edge and back (5 miles)
Cleeve Hill to Brockhampton and back (12 miles)
Cleeve Hill to Belas Knap and Winchcombe and back (8 miles)

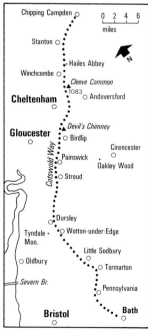

Leckhampton to Coldwell Bottom and back (6 miles)
Cleeve Common circular (5 miles)
Birdlip to Brockworth and back (5½ miles)
Charlton Kings to Andoversford and back (12 miles)

● Chipping Campden

There are a number of good circular walks near the town:
Dovers Hill and Aston Hill (3½ miles)
Dovers Hill, Saintbury and Willersey (7½ miles)
Campden Railway Tunnel and Mickleton Hills Farm (2½ miles)
The Mile Drive and Broadway Tower (7 miles)
Broad Campden and Campden Hills Farm (2½ miles)

● Cirencester

There is a fine 3,000-acre park here with avenues of chestnut trees. Walk from the park to Sapperton through Oakley Wood, and then on to Chalford.

Fields near Chipping Campden with a typical Cotswold stone farmhouse.

● Forest of Dean

There are 22,000 acres of woodland, and some evidence of the once-prosperous mining industry remains. A few small coal mines are still worked. These forest trails are suggested:
Christchurch Forest Trail (3 miles), off B4432 and B4228
Biblins Forest Trail (4 miles), off B4432 north of Christchurch
Abbotswood Forest Trail (3 miles), near the Soudleys

● Painswick

A fascinating 3-mile walk runs along Painswick Stream, past a number of mills. The town itself is on the edge of a wooded valley.

● Wotton-under-Edge

There is a pleasant 8-mile walk from the end of Market Street to Kingswood, Wortley and Blackquarries Hill, past the Tyndale Monument and back down past Brackenbury Ditches, the remains of an Iron Age encampment.

OS maps: 149, 150, 151, 162, 163

Hereford and Worcester

The North Worcestershire Path

Essential Information

Length: 15 miles, from the Lickey Hills Country Park at Beacon Hill to Kingsford Country Park, near Kidderminster.
Going: easy
OS maps: 138, 139

The Path links four Country Parks in the north-eastern corner of the old county of Worcestershire. The start is at the Lickey Hills Country Park at Beacon Hill, and the Path moves down through oak woodland to open fields and then into the Waseley Hills Country Park, where it rises to nearly 900 feet on the high grasslands, with contrasting views down to Birmingham and the Severn Valley. Woodland gives way to arable land and then a valley bottom brings the walker into the Clent Hills Country Park. The Hills are 500 to 1,000 feet high and again provide superb views. Then the route passes Hagley Hall and runs cross-country to the River Stour, finally reaching Kingsford Country Park, 2? acres of mixed forest and birch woodland, 3 miles north of Kidderminster.

● The Wychavon Way

Essential Information

Length: 40 miles, from Holt Fleet on the River Severn to Winchcombe in the Cotswolds.
Going: easy
OS map: 150

The Way starts at the bridging-point of the Severn at Holt Fleet. Parklands and the village of Ombersley follow, as well as the view of the stately home of Westwood Park. The spa town of Droitwich, where the Romans mined salt, contains many fine Victorian buildings. The path continues along the Roman Salt Way and a canal towpath to come, by remote country lanes, to the Lenches, a series of hills with views of the Malverns. Then it runs through the orchard belt of the Vale of Evesham, crosses the Avon and achieves Bredon Hill, with a magnificent view of the Avon Valley and the Cotswolds. At the end, the path climbs the Alderton and Langley Hills to Winchcombe, where it meets the Cotswold Way (see page 70), just north-east of Cheltenham.

Suggested Walking Areas

● The Clent Hills

The Clent Hills Country Park consists of 365 acres of grassland hill country of great interest to the ornithologist. There are splendid views of the surrounding countryside from the many footpaths that connect Adams Hill, Walton Hill and the Four Stones.

Map showing the Wychavon Way. Locations marked: Kingsford, Kidderminster, Clent Hills ▲1034, Ombersley, Holt Fleet, Lickey Hills ▲, Droitwich, Worcester, Malvern Hills ▲1394, ▲1114, ▲ Midsummer Hill, ▲ Bredon Hill, Winchcombe. Scale: 0 2 4 6 miles. N.

above: Symond's Yat.
below: View south to Midsummer Hill.

Hergest Ridge

Walks from the second turning left off the A44 Kington to Rhayader road give fine views from the north side of the ridge.

The Malvern Hills

There are magnificent views of the Malverns from Herefordshire Beacon which rises to 1,114 feet. On the summit is a very fine Iron Age hill fort. There is a good path from the A449 Ledbury to Malvern road. A superb climbing walk leads from the A438 between Ledbury and Tewkesbury to Midsummer Hill and panoramic views of the Cotswolds and the Welsh mountains.

Symond's Yat

5 miles south of Ross-on-Wye on the B4229:

Symond's Yat forest walk: 1 mile with 1¾-mile extension to Coldwell Rocks.

High Meadow circular path, a fine 10-mile walk through the Wye Valley. Landmarks are Symond's Yat, King Arthur's Rocks, Seven Sisters Rock, Christchurch Camp and the ecological reserve.

OS maps: 137, 138, 139, 148, 149, 150, 161, 162

Shropshire

Offa's Dyke Path (see pages 64-67) runs through the south and north-western edges of the county and offers some fine walking.

Suggested Walking Areas

● Caer Caradoc

From Church Stretton a footpath runs 2 miles north-east to the 1,506-foot summit of Caer Caradoc. Some 750 feet up is the cave where the British leader Caractacus made his last stand against the Romans in AD50.

● The Clee Hills

These hills lie a little north-east of Ludlow. Both the main summits – Titterstone Clee (1,750 feet) and Brown Clee (1,790 feet) – offer a good climb, and there are many other footpath walks.

● The Long Mynd

West of Church Stretton, this ridge of hills is 10 miles long and encloses over 4,000 acres of moor and heath. The Port Way, an ancient track, runs along the crest of the ridge, giving superb views of the Shropshire countryside. A good walk on to the ridge is through the lovely Cardingmill Valley.

● Stiperstones

There is another ridge path, 2 to 3 miles long, here, and footpaths run up to the 1,700-foot summit.

● Wenlock Edge

This limestone ridge, immortalized in A.E. Housman's *Shropshire Lad*, runs for some 16 miles south-westwards from the town of Much Wenlock. There are fine walks and good views everywhere.

The Long Mynd.

● The Wrekin

This isolated hill provides a fine footpath climb to the 1,334-foot summit.

● Wyre Forest

There are delightful walks along the forest borders from the charming village of Kinlet. A particularly leafy one runs to Baveney Wood. The Green Walk runs from the Visitor Centre at Callow Hill along the escarpment, commanding views of the forest and the Clee Hills.

OS maps: 117, 118, 126, 127, 137, 138

View from the Stiperstones.

Gwent

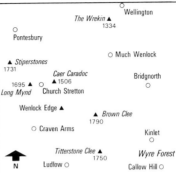

The Usk Valley Walk

Essential Information

Length: 23 miles, from Caerleon to Abergavenny
Going: easy
OS maps: 161, 171

This Walk runs through delightful country along the banks of the River Usk, famous for its salmon and trout fishing. Villages, hamlets and lanes alternate with stretches of lovely river walks. Near the 18th-century Kemeys Folly there are good views, and 18th-century Usk is worth a visit. Next come the windmill at Llancayo, superb views from Coed-y-Bwnydd and Clytha Castle, built in 1790, before Abergavenny, with its now-ruined 14th-century castle, is reached.

Suggested Walking Areas

● Barbadoes Forest Walk

Heavy walking through the forest with views over the lower Wye valley (2 miles).

● Monmouth – Brecon Canal

The towpath along the 30-mile canal is a fascinating walk.

● Mynydd Du Forest Walk

Easy 1½-mile forest trail

The Brecon and Abergavenny Canal.

through Ffavyddog Wood, beginning 2½ miles north-west of Partrishaw.

● St Marys Nature Trail

Starts ½ mile west of Llwyn Du Reservoir, on the Brecon road out of Abergavenny. It is 2 miles up a steep valley on to Sugar Loaf Hill and the moorland of the Brecon Beacons.

● The Tintern Chapel Hill Forest Walk

Easy 1½-mile walk in 7 marked stages. Combined with a visit to the Abbey, the walk makes a good family outing.

OS maps: 161, 162, 171

South Glamorgan

Suggested Walking Areas

● Barry

There are many walks in the 250-acre Porthkerry Country Park and a fine valley descending to the sea at Porthkerry Bay. Bull Path along the cliff edge is an interesting walk.

● Cardiff

The 5-mile **Taff Valley Walk** begins at the north gate of the Castle and runs through the grounds to the nature reserve along the Glamorgan Canal.

The **Bute Park Nature Trail** is a 2-mile route through Bute Park, from the castle to Blackweir.

The **Nant Fawr Walk** is a 3-mile path following the Nant Fawr Brook through Cardiff.

● Llandaff

The Canton to Llandaff Walk is a 3-mile route through Victoria and Thompsons Parks to Llandaff Court.

● Rhymney

The Rhymney Walk runs for 3 miles through Hill Gardens Rhymney.

● Welsh St Donats

Two pleasant forest walks through a delightful vale start from the A4222 north of Aberithin.

● Wenallt Hill

There are two 1-mile nature trails on Wenallt Hill 5½ miles north of Cardiff on the Caerphilly road.

OS maps: 170, 171

Dare Valley, Aberdare.

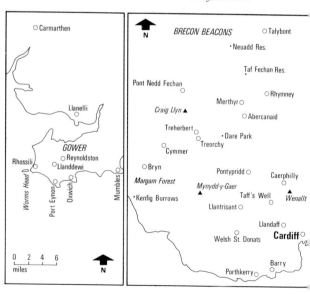

Mid-Glamorgan

The Coed Morgannwg Way (see page 78) runs for a short way through the county.

Ffordd y Bryniau (Ridgeway Walk)

Essential Information

Length: 21 miles, from Mynydd y Gaer to Caerphilly Common
Going: relatively easy
OS maps: 170, 171

This is a walk through varied landscape chiefly along ancient hill tracks, but also on urban footpaths and forest paths in the valleys. From Mynydd y Gaer the path runs through Llantrisant Forest into Llantrisant, a pleasant hill town, past The Caerau, an Iron Age hill fort, and tumuli on Garth Hill to Taff's Well Spa, the only thermal spring in Wales. The final stretch of the Walk is to Caerphilly Common, a short way outside the town.

Suggested Walking Areas

● Abercanaid

The 4-mile Old Glamorgan Canal Walk runs through the Taff Valley alongside the now disused canal.

● Brecon Beacons

The Brecon Beacons National Park falls in Mid-Glamorgan and in Powys. Recommended walks in Mid-Glamorgan are: **Garwnant Forest Walk** (2 miles) from the Forest Centre **Talybont Forest** walks (1 mile, two of 2 miles, one of 3 miles) through the woodland around the headwaters of the Caefanell River **Pont Cwm-y-Fedwen Forest Walk** (2 miles) through the Taf Fechan Valley **Taf Fechan** walk (10 miles) from Taf Fechan reservoir to Neuadd reservoirs and back

● Dare Valley

A 3-mile stretch of the old **Brecon and Merthyr Tydfil Junction Railway** can be walked between Cwmaman and the Dare Valley Country Park.
The **Country Park** also has a number of walks between 1 and 5 miles long.

● Kenfig Burrows

A 3-mile nature trail runs from Kenfig along the superb beach to the Burrows, a wild dune-land area.

● Mynydd Beili-Glas

Mynydd-Beili-Glas on the A4061 between Treherbert to Hirwaun road is the starting point for two walks.
The 2½-mile **Griag Lyn Ridge Walk** runs along the ridge separating the Rhondda and the Aberdare and Neath Valleys. The 4-mile **Lluest Walk** heads east to Lluestwen reservoir.

● Pontypridd

There are 3 miles of paths on Mynydd Eglwysilan with good views of the Taff and Rhondda Valleys.

● Treherbert

Starting 3 miles north of Treherbert the Blaen Rhondda Walk runs for 2 to 3 miles through the Upper Rhondda Valley.

● Treorchy

There are 3 walks on the hills around Treorchy, two of 5 to 6 miles, one of 7 to 8 miles.

OS maps: 160, 161, 170, 171

West Glamorgan

The Coed Morgannwg Way

Essential Information

Length: 27 miles, from Craig y Llyn to Margam Country Park
Going: relatively easy, with some ascents and descents
OS map: 170

Coed Morgannwg is the collective name for three forests, Cymmer, Rheola and Margam, and it is through these three, which together constitute the largest forested area in Wales, and through a small part of the Rhondda Forest that the Way runs.

From the start at Craid y Llyn, a viewpoint in the Rhondda Forest, the path follows first the ridge between the Afan and Neath Valleys and then the one between Cymmer and Rheola Forests. At Carn Caglau the Way begins to drop but then climbs again to Mynydd Rhiw Cregan, where there are splendid views.

Another descent and another climb follow, to Garn Wen, 1,182 feet up. The last section of the path runs through Bryn and then through mature woodland into Margam Country Park.

Suggested Walking Areas

● The Gower Peninsula

There are superb beaches, high cliffs and wooded valleys on this beautiful peninsula, plus a wide variety of walks. Especially recommended are:

Oxwich

A 1-mile nature trail runs along Oxwich Sands.

Oxwich-Crawley Woods

This 6-mile circular walk starts at the car park at Oxwich. Walk along the fine beach to the church and on to the woods where the dunes finish. Follow

Rhossili Bay.

The Knave, Port-Eynon.

the path beside the stream up through the woods to the road on the cliff top, and then follow the road back to Oxwich.

Worms Head

Worms Head is the further-most of two tiny islands off the far west coast of Gower. There is a good walk from Rhossili to the shore, and the Devil's Bridge, a causeway over the rocks, can be followed at certain tides.

A 3-mile nature trail also runs from Rhossili.

Reynoldston

Arthur's Stone is reached from the village on a 1-mile path uphill and across moorland. The Stone is a cromlech 14 feet long, 6 wide and 8 thick.

Llanddewi

Three farm trails, of 2, 5½ and 6 miles, start from the village.

Port-Eynon

The Port-Eynon Point Walk is a 2¾-mile route through a National Trust reserve. There is interesting bird life and marvellous views.

● Pont Nedd Fechan to Brecon

This is a 20-mile walk over the Brecon Beacons, via Middle and Upper Clun-gwny Falls, Ystradfellte and Heol Senni.

● Vale of Neath

This is a delightful area, with a number of gorges and water-falls. About 1¼ miles from Pont Nedd Fechan a path leads to the Ysgwd Gwladys (Lady Fall). A longer route on the other side of the river leads to Ysgwd Einon Gam. Another worthwhile fall, Ysgwd-yr-Eira, is reached in about 1¼ hours from Pont Nedd Fechan over Craig-y-Dinas.

OS maps: 159, 160, 170

Dyfed

The major walk in Dyfed is the Pembrokeshire Coast Path (see page 68). Particularly attractive short sections on the Path are from Bosherton to Elegug Stack (5 miles), on Dinas Island, which is really a headland, and around Tenby, at Waterwynch, Giltar Point and Lydstep Head.

Suggested Walking Areas

● Borth

The 12-mile Ynyslas Nature Trails run through duneland in the Ynyslas Nature Reserve, 7 miles north of Aberystwyth.

● The Cambrian Mountains

There is good, firm walking in the Plynlimon group of mountains. The easy climb up Plynlimon Fawr, at 2,468 feet the highest in the group, starts 5 miles east of Devil's Bridge on the A44 at Eisteddfa. The path follows an old leadminers' track to the top. It can be a difficult walk in bad weather, but on a fine day the views across the mountains to Shropshire are magnificent.

● Clarbeston

The 7½-mile Lysfran Reservoir

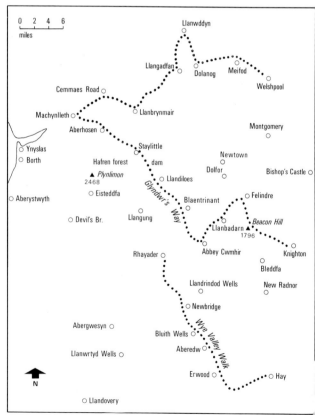

Country Park Walk winds round the edge of the reservoir, offering the chance to observe natural life on land and water.

● Devil's Bridge

The Devil's Bridge Nature Trail (1 mile) runs from the junction of the A4120 and the B4574, through woods, steep at times, with fine waterfalls.

● Hafod

Three short trails through the Hafod estate, now run by the Forestry Commission, show the landscaping schemes of Thomas Jones, with terraces and exotic trees. The estate lies 2 miles south-east of Devil's Bridge on the B4574.

● The Presely Hills

In prehistoric times these hills provided the stones for Stonehenge. Although they are only 1,760 feet at the highest point, there are fine views and on a clear day Ireland can be seen. A 6-mile path from Croesfihangel passes prehistoric remains: a lovely remote walk.

OS maps: 135, 145, 146, 147, 157, 158, 159, 160

River gorge above Devil's Bridge.

Powys

Offa's Dyke Path (see pages 64-67) runs through the county near the English border.

Glyndwr's Way

Essential Information

Length: 120 miles, from Knighton to Welshpool
Going: varied, from easy to heavy
OS maps: 125, 126, 135, 136, 148

Named for Owen Glyndwr, the celebrated Welsh leader and warrior who led the struggle against England in the early 15th century, this walk runs in a three-quarter circle through Powys, passing near many places associated with him.

The start is at Knighton, also midway point of Offa's Dyke Path. The first target is Llancoch, reached across easy country lanes and farm tracks. The Way then crosses Short

Ditch, a rampart built by the English in 1402 as a forward defence against Glyndwr, and climbs across moorland towards Beacon Hill. After Felindre the path is easier again to Llanbadarn Fynydd past Bronze Age tumuli, and then there is high ridge walking until the descent to Neuadd Fach Wood and Abbey Cwmhir (28 miles).

The land is wilder now, with good views, as the walker heads for Blaentrinant and Llanidloes. An easier stretch past old mine workings to Staylittle is next, past Clywedog Dam and along the attractive Llyn Clywedog Valley. But this precedes the section to Aberhosan (60½ miles) which runs across hostile moorland in the Plynlimon foothills. At Machynlleth Owen Glyndwr held his Parliament, was

crowned Prince of Wales and planned the establishment of an independent Wales. Several ascents and descents continue the path to Cemmaes Road, and then there is easier walking to Llanbrynmair. Now comes one of the wildest sections of the Way across hills and moorland to Llangadfan (89½ miles). Forests follow to Llanwddyn and then an easy walk on to Dolanog. The last section is a pleasant walk through Meifod to Welshpool, where Offa's Dyke Path is again met.

The Kerry Ridgeway

Essential Information

Length: 15½ miles, from Dolfor, near Newton, to Bishops Castle
Going: easy
OS maps: 136, 137

Claimed to be the oldest pathway in Wales, the Kerry Ridge-

left: The Elan Valley, near Rhayader.
above: Hay Bluff, near Glasbury-on-Wye.

way follows the crest of the Kerry Hills. It is a fascinating walk, with wide views and past many archaeological remains, including Iron Age dykes and Bronze Age barrows. At the eastern end, Bishopsmoat is a motte and bailey castle strategically placed at a narrow point on the Ridgeway.

The Wye Valley Walk

Essential Information

Length: 36 miles, from Hay-on-Wye to Rhayader
Going: easy, mostly along the river bank, with some climbs
OS maps: 147, 148, 161

From Hay – a fascinating border town with Monday cattle sales and pony sales each autumn, plus a wealth of second-hand

83

Forestry plantations near Abergwesyn.

bookshops – the walker follows the river bank for most of the way to Erwood, although the stretch from Llowes to Glasbury is on higher ground. From Erwood to Builth Wells most of the Walk runs on high ground again, past Aberedw Rocks and near Llewelyn's Cave, where, so tradition has it, Llewelyn hid from the English. The stretch to Newbridge follows the river at first, then runs through wooded hills. The last section of the path is chiefly on high ground again, with good views of the Wye and Elan Valleys.

Suggested Walking Areas

● Abbey Cwmhir

A 7-mile route leads between Y Glog and Little Park, then east-north-east to Porth and south-west back to the banks of the Cwm Cynydd and down the valley to the starting-point.

● Abergwesyn

There are several short walks in the Cwm Irfon Forest near Llanwrtyd Wells.

● Bleddfa

There is a pleasant 8-mile trail through Bleddfa Forest.

● Llandovery

An 8-mile route takes the walker north through the Cwm y Rhaiadr plantation to Troed-y-rhiw-fer. The return is by the same path or along the road.

● Llandrindod Wells

This spa town is the starting-point for a 7-mile circular walk through woodland to Shaky Bridge and on to Cwm.

● Llangurig

A good 4-mile track walk runs south-east to Bodtalog and then north-north-east to Pentgwynhill.

● Llanidloes

The Llyn Clwedog Scenic Trail runs for 2½ miles near the shore of Clwedog reservoir.
Hafren Forest boasts six good walks:
Cascades Forest Trail (1 mile)
Hafren Falls Walk (3¾ miles)
Hore-Tanllwyth Walk (3¾ miles)
Maesnant Walk (3 miles)
Severn-Nant Ricket Walk (3½ miles)
Severn-Plynlimon-Garreg Wen Walk (8 miles)

● Llanwrtyd Wells

A hard 9-mile walk runs via Nant-yr-odin to Nant-y-cerdin and Bwlchmawr.

● New Radnor

Past the site of the castle, a 7-mile walk skirts Whimble Hill, passes the end of Whinyard Rocks. It then rounds the head of the valley and runs back to the starting-point via Ferndale and Knowle Hill.

OS maps: 124, 125, 135, 136, 137, 147, 148, 160, 161

Clwyd

The best long-distance walking in Clwyd is along Offa's Dyke Path (see pages 64-67).

Suggested Walking Areas

● Llangollen

An easy 10-mile walk from Chirk to Llangollen along an arm of the Shropshire Union canal. Chirk Castle (1310) is fine, the countryside superb. The Pontcysyllte Aqueduct, which carries the canal over the River Dee, is the highlight of the walk.

● Colwyn Bay

The Bryn Euryn Nature Trail winds for 1½ miles from Rhos on Sea to Mochdre. There are fine views of Snowdonia and the coast and much interesting flora and fauna.

● Holywell Nature Trail

A pleasant 3-mile river-valley walk through woods and past the 12th century Abbey of Basingwerk. The Trail starts east of the Pen-y-Maes Estate off the A5026.

● Moel Fammau Trail

East of Ruthin take the B5429 north to the Clwyd Forest. The 4-mile walk begins on a way-marked path through the forest, then climbs over moor-land to the summit of the Clwydian hills (1820 feet). There are marvellous views over the vale of Clwyd, fascinating plants, birds and trees.

● Mold

The Moel Arthur Country Park is set in the Clwydian Hills. Offa's Dyke Path runs through, and there are numerous short walks, with an Iron Age hill fort, nature trails, and fine views of the vale of Clwyd.

● Prestatyn

The Bishopswood Nature Trail is an easy 2-miles, beginning above St Melyd golf course south of Prestatyn. There is superb woodland walking, with views to Anglesey, Snowdon, Llandudno and Great Orme.

OS maps: 116, 117, 125, 126

The River Dee near Llangollen.

Gwynedd

Suggested Walking Areas

● Barmouth

There is a splendid 4-mile Panorama Walk with views of Cader Idris, the Diffwys range and the Mawddach Estuary.

● Beddgelert

There are numerous forest walks through majestic scenery.
Beddgelert Forest, four walks between ½ and 3 miles
Cae Dafydd Forest Walk (2 miles)
A tough 8-mile walk runs to Llyn Dinas and Hafod Owen, Nantmor and back through the Aberglaslyn Pass.

● Betws-y-Coed

There are ten walks in the Gwydyr Forest:
Church Walk (¾ mile)
Cyrau Walk (2 miles)
Llugwy Gorge (4½ miles)
Plateau Walk (4 miles)
Drws Gwyn (3 miles)
Llyn Sarnau (5¼ miles)
Craig Forys (1¾ miles)
Llyn Glangors (2¼ miles)
Artist's Wood (1½ miles)
Chapel Walk (¾ mile)
The **Gwydyr Forest Trail** runs for 3 miles from Ty Hyll to Miners Bridge
A 6-mile walk runs north to Llyn y Parc, west and south to Diosgydd and to Miners Bridge

Snowdon from Capel Curig.

● Cader Idris

A number of paths run up Wales' second highest peak, from whose top there are magnificent views.
The Pony Track (easy) and **Foxes' Path** (less easy) both lead up from the car park at the end of Gwernan Lake.

● Capel Curig

The Cwm Idwal Nature Trail runs through the Cwm Idwal National Nature Reserve for 2 miles.

● Dolgellau

The Precipice Walk runs for 3 miles around the mountain ridge, starting 2½ miles north of the town on the Llanfachreth road.

● Ganllwyd

Two 2-mile forest trails, the **Dolgefeiliau Forest Trail** and the **Ty'n-y-Groes Forest Trail** start from Ganllwyd.

● Holyhead

The Penrhos Nature Trail runs for 5 miles along the coast and through woodlands.

● Llanberis

A 6-mile walk runs from the Country Park to Hafodty, then to Dinorwic and Fachwen, returning through woodland to the Country Park.

● Llandudno

The Great Orme Nature Trail is a magnificent 5-mile walk along Great Orme Head with good views.

● Llanfairfechan

The Coedydd Aber Nature Trail (3 miles) leads to the Aber Falls from Bontnewydd village.

● Maentwrog

There is a 2-3 mile nature trail – starting on the B4410 to Rhyd.

● Newborough

There are six paths, between 2 and 4 miles, through the Ynys Llanddwyn National Nature Reserve on Anglesey.

● Penmaenpool

A disused railway is the site for a 7-mile walk from Penmaenpool to Morfa Mawddach along the previously inaccessible shore of the Mawddach Estuary.

● Snowdon

The centrepiece of the Snowdonia National Park can be climbed along two main paths:
The Pyg Track, along the north west ridge from the Pen-y-Pass youth hostel
The Miners' Track, also starting from the youth hostel but running across Llyn Llydaw and through Glaslyn
The two paths together make a good 8-mile circular walk.

● Trawsfynydd

The Trawsfynydd Nature Trail makes a 3-mile circuit of the shore of Llyn Trawsfynydd.

OS maps: 114, 115, 116, 123, 124, 125, 135

87

The Midlands and East Anglia

For the walker, the attractions of the central and eastern counties of England are not always as immediately obvious as they should be. But there is much good walking here even if the terrain is less glamorous and more gentle than in other regions.

Not that the area lacks excitement. The Staffordshire Moorlands, for instance, only a short distance from the built-up mass of the West Midlands, are a high and wild area, with plenty of challenging walks. Elsewhere, the pleasures of the landscape are kinder but no less genuine: the mature parklands of Northamptonshire, dotted with yellow stone villages; Leicester and Nottingham, rolling shire counties with fine forests and mellow villages.

And there are the flatlands of East Anglia: wide, open skies with scudding clouds and fine sunsets, grain-filled fields and, surprisingly often, softly rolling hills, contrasting

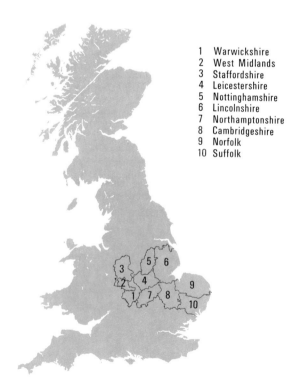

1 Warwickshire
2 West Midlands
3 Staffordshire
4 Leicestershire
5 Nottinghamshire
6 Lincolnshire
7 Northamptonshire
8 Cambridgeshire
9 Norfolk
10 Suffolk

he marshes, Broads and river estuaries.

There are no official long-distance paths in this section. But the West Midland Way makes an interesting 140-mile circuit of the West Midlands conurbation through surprisingly varied terrain, a refreshing route within easy reach for a day's outing.

These, then, are the secret pleasures of middle England – not the drama of the south-west or the north, but the very essence of the English landscape and ideal walking country.

Practical Points on Leisure Walking

● Work out your route carefully beforehand – even a short afternoon stroll can be spoiled if unnecessary detours have to be made.

● Park your car safely, and legally, at the start of a walk. A local pub or in the vicinity of a police station (preferably with prior notice) is a good choice.

● Be especially careful if your route crosses land grazed by bulls.

Do not allow children or elderly people to walk near the animals.

● It is a sensible precaution to carry a sweater or jacket and probably a waterproof even on a summer walk – the British weather is not predictable!

● Sensible and comfortable footwear will add greatly to the pleasure and, in some circumstances, the safety of a walk.

West Midland Way

Essential Information

Length: 162 miles, in a circular route through Worcestershire, Warwickshire, Staffordshire and Shropshire
Going: easy
Terrain: varied, including canal tow-paths, hills, woodland and moorland
OS maps: 126, 127, 138, 139, 150, 151

The West Midland Way describes an irregular circle around the populous and industrialized West Midlands and can easily be reached for weekend or day outings. The Way is full of scenic and historic interest and makes an ideal starting-ground for serious walking. For the most part it follows country tracks and pathways away from the roads. Being a circular walk, the Way can be started anywhere – but perhaps most aptly at Meriden, where the medieval cross on the green marks the centre of England.

Meriden to Kenilworth: 8¾ miles

The Way climbs through field to Berkswell and continues to Kenilworth Castle, started in 1112 with further additions in 1162. Ruined during the Civil War, it is none the less still an impressive sight.

Kenilworth to Henley-in-Arden: 11 miles

This is a lovely section, easy going past Honiley Church and the Boot Inn (1470) to Wroxall. After crossing the Grand Union Canal, continue through woodland to the cast-iron bridge over the Stratford-on-Avon Canal. Now there is canal walking to Lock 36, then past the old barn near Preston Bragot and on to Kite Green.

Henley-in-Arden to Adams Hill: 22 miles

This stretch is often wooded, the country undulating, the walking conditions good. Ullenhall and Alvechurch villages make pleasant resting-points, and there are fine views from Hob and Lickey Hills. It is lovely countryside around the Worcester and Birmingham Canal, and Beacon Hill gives panoramic views over Wenlock Edge, the Malverns and the Cotswolds. At Highfield there are more views before Waseley Country Park. Then the Way runs over Windmill Hill to Clent Hill, offering wide views over the centre of England. The section ends at Adams Hill, where there is an unusual double-towered folly.

Adams Hill to Bridgnorth: 25 miles

The path crosses the Staffordshire and Worcestershire Canal and the River Stour and at Kinver Edge goes through fine woods into Staffordshire. Above Kinver Village make a detour to Holy Austin Rock, where caves are carved out of the rock.

After Kinver the lush parkland of Sheepwalks leads to a fine section at Lakehouse Dingle, with woods and a waterfall. Then cross the Severn by ferry at Hampton Loade. After good field walks the Way arrives at Bridgnorth, where the 12th-century castle with its leaning keep should be visited.

Bridgnorth to Brocton: 37 miles

The highlights of this stretch are the old mill wheel on the River Worfe, Worfield Village, Tong, where Dickens set *The*

Bridgnorth and the Severn Valley.

Old Curiosity Shop, White Ladies Priory, The Royal Oak at Boscobel, where Charles I hid after the Battle of Worcester and the Norman convent of Black Ladies. The walking is easy and the history fascinating.

Brocton to Whittington: 27 miles

The wild 30,000 acres of Cannock Chase makes this part of the Way a marvellous walk. Once a royal hunting-ground, the Chase is now a preserved area. Landmarks to note are the triumphal arch at Shugborough, the 17th-century Shugborough Hall, the Forestry Commission Museum and Information Centre at Birches Valley, and Castle Ring, the highest point of Cannock Chase.

Whittington to Meriden: 32 miles

The Way continues along easy tracks. There are views from Roundhill Wood, and then comes Middleton village, a stiled footbridge at Langley Brook, and Kingsbury. On the last stretch back to Meriden, take care near Kingsbury rifle range. The villages are pretty, and more fine views await just before Maxstoke with its 14th-century church and priory remains. Meriden lies ahead, the circle of the Way complete.

91

Warwickshire

The West Midlands Way runs through the county as part of its circuit of the West Midlands conurbation (see pages 90-91).

Suggested Walking Areas

● Burton Dasset Hills

There is a short trail here over the five peaks through unspoilt grassland country.

● Compton Wynyates

This is one of the most splendid of the country houses in all Britain, a masterpiece of Tudor architecture, with scarcely any later additions. The path from Compton Wynyates to Upper Tysoe complements this magnificence, with splendid views over the Warwickshire plain.

● Earlswood

A 2-mile trail from New Fallings Coppice runs through oakwood and past Earlswood reservoir and interesting marshes.

● Edge Hill

This is the site of the first battle of the English Civil War, in 1642, and there is a pleasant short walk along the escarpment through woods and fields.

● Newbold Comyn

A 5-mile trail runs from Leamington Spa through the Country Park. There is varied wildlife and good views from Observation Hill.

● Stratford-upon-Avon Canal

The canal towpath is an excellent walk. The 4-mile stretch from Lapworth to Lowsonford and back is especially recommended.

● Welcombe Hills

A 2-mile nature trail from the outskirts of Stratford-upon-Avon over woodland and grassland and with good views and interesting flora and fauna.

OS maps: 139, 140, 150, 151

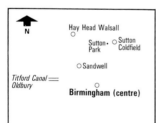

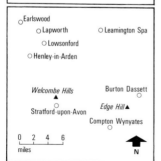

Compton Wynyates.

West Midlands

Part of the Titford Canal which opened in 1837.

Suggested Walking Areas

● Bracebridge Nature Trail

A fine 2-mile walk through Sutton Park, circling Bracebridge Pool. The scenery and wildlife are varied.

● Forest of Arden

Henley-in-Arden is the focus for several fine walks, through rolling country beside the River Alne in the heart of the old forest.

● Haden Hill Park Trail

2 miles of parkland and small lakes starting from Haden Hill House.

● Hay Head

This short trail follows the last stretch of the Hay Head branch of the Wyrley and Essington Canal and leads into a 2-mile walk on to Walsall.

● Longmoor Nature Trail

A 2-mile circular walk in Sutton Park, Sutton Coldfield. Look out for varied flora, from marsh plants to fir and pine trees, and a stretch of Roman road.

● Sandwell Valley Recreational Park

There are two walks, the Hawk Trail (1½ miles) and the Duck Trail (¾ mile). Both pass the site of Sandwell Hall, an old Benedictine monastery and two large lakes and woodlands, where wildlife abounds.

● The Titford Canal Walk

A short but fascinating walk of nearly 2 miles along the Titford Canal, which is part of the Birmingham Canal Navigation. The start is at Oldbury Junction. Then the towpath passes six locks and under several interesting bridges to reach the Titford Pools. An engine house and an early 19th-century forge are passed along the way.

OS maps: 128, 138, 139, 140

93

Staffordshire

The Staffordshire Way

Essential Information

Length: 59 miles, from Congleton Edge to Cannock Chase

Going: variable with some easy lowland stretches and quite tough on Cannock Chase

OS maps: 118, 126

The Way moves from Congleton Edge into the Cheshire plain, through the valleys of the Churnet, the Dove and the Trent to end at Cannock Chase. It consists of footpaths, towpaths, hilltop tracks and fields. The path follows the gritstone ridge between the Pennines and the Cheshire Plain to reach the Cloud, a cliff offering splendid views to the Welsh hills, then wooded slopes to Rudyard Lake and to Leek, gateway to the Peaks.

The towpath along the Caldon Canal brings the Way into Churnet valley and then over fields to Alton. The town of Rocester offers historic interest from Roman times to the Industrial Revolution, and from here the Way continues along the Dove Valley to Uttoxeter, through woodland to Abbots Bromley and on to Blithfield Reservoir with its teeming birdlife. The Trent Valley at Colwich brings the Way together with the Trent and Mersey Canal and two historic railways. Then comes Shugborough Hall, a magnificent 18th-century mansion house and finally Cannock Chase. It is hoped to extend the Way by mid-1983 along a 35-mile section to Kinver Edge where it will connect with the North Worcestershire Way (see pages 72-73).

Suggested Walking Areas

● Cannock Chase

30,000 acres of moorland and the remnants of the medieval royal forest give superb views on walks along the Severn Springs over Oakedge Park and Abraham's Valley. The walk from Milford to Sher brook Ford through delightful leafy slopes has views of the Satnall Hills. Walking may be difficult, and map and compass are required.

● Staffordshire Moorlands

A series of 12 circular walks through the Staffordshire Moorlands, most connecting with the Staffordshire Way.

Threapwood: three alternative short walks around Threap Wood and Ousal Dale, (maximum 2½ miles), with views of the Churnet Valley and Alton Towers.

Cotton and Oakmoor: a pleasant 3-mile walk, north of Oakamoor with excellent views of Cotton Dell. The going ca

Congleton Edge / The Cloud / The Roaches / ▲ Hen Cloud / ○ Meerbrook / ○ Rudyard ● / ○ Leek / Biddulph ○ / Cheddleton ○ / ○ Ipstones / Consall ○ / ○ Froghall / Kingsley ○ / ○ Oakmoor / Cheadle ○ / Threapwood / Alton ○ / Rocester ○ / Uttoxeter ○ ● / Abbots Bromley ○ / Shugborough ○ ● ○ Colwich / Cannock Chase / N / 0 2 4 6 / miles

often be wet and very muddy.

Froghall and Foxt: 4 miles through beautiful woodlands between Froghall and Foxt, taking in the old lime kilns at Froghall Wharf.

Ipstones: 5 miles through fields and mine-workings around the village of Ipstone, one of the birthplaces of the industrial revolution.

Kingsley and Consall Forge: a strenuous 4-mile tramp through woodlands and the secluded Churnet valley, north of Kingsley.

Cheadle: 7½ miles of track and field through woodland and farmland around the town of Cheadle. The going may be wet.

Cheddleton: a 7-mile circular path east of Cheddleton through the Combes Valley and Nature Reserve, past 17th-century buildings at Sharpcliffe Hall and Whitehough.

Leek: 9 miles on country paths around Leek with high woodlands and the abundant wildlife of the Churnet Valley.

Rudyard Lake: an easy 4-mile walk along footpaths and old railway track through the wooded slopes circling lovely Rudyard Lake.

Tittesworth and Meerbrook: 7½ miles of often wet walking around Tittesworth Reservoir, through the villages of Meerbrook and Middle Hume.

The Roaches and Hen Cloud: a strenuous climbing walk for 5½ miles along the massive millstone outcrop of the Roaches.

Biddulph: 10½ miles around Biddulph with superb views from Congleton Edge over much of the Cheshire Plain.

OS maps: 118, 119, 127, 128, 129

Cannock Chase.

Leicestershire

The southernmost section of the Viking Way runs through Leicestershire (see page 100).

The Jubilee Way

Essential Information

Length: 15½ miles, from Melton Mowbray to Brewer's Grave, where it meets the Viking Way
Going: easy, but often muddy
OS maps: 129, 130

The Jubilee Way starts across softly rolling pasture land and through woodland stretches between Melton Mowbray and Scalford. From here the route passes over farming land to higher ground at Goadby Marwood, then crosses iron-stone mining country and runs along a pre-Roman road, used for transporting salt, to Eaton (8½ miles). Next there are 6 miles through the woodlands of the Belvoir Estate before Belvoir Castle is reached (the predecessors of the present early 19th-century structure date back to the 11th century). The last section of the Way passes through magnificent parkland before crossing the River Devon near Woolsthorpe to Brewer's Grave, on the Viking Way.

Suggested Walking Areas

● Beacon Hill

Several waymarked footpaths take the walker up Beacon Hill (853 feet) where there are views over the Trent and Soar Valleys.

● Bosworth Battlefield

The Battle Trail takes walkers round the site of the Battle of Bosworth Field, fought on 22 August 1485. Here the Wars of the Roses came to an end, and the Tudor dynasty was established on the English throne.

● Bradgate Park

800 acres of mixed country with good walking through parts of Charnwood Forest, the Lin Valley and moorland. The Park includes the ruins of Bradgate House, once home of Lady Jane Grey.

● Burrough Hill

One of the highest points in east Leicestershire, the hill is topped by an Iron Age hill fort. The Dalby Hills Path runs for over a mile through pleasant country from the hill.

● Groby Pool

A footpath joins Groby village with the county's largest natural

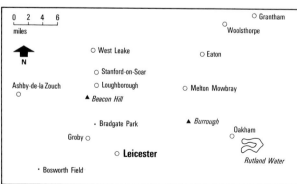

e and its rich and varied
ldlife.

The Moira Trail

king its name from a local
ndowner, this 2½-mile walk
ar Ashby-de-la-Zouch recalls
e early 19th century, when
e area was a flourishing coal-
ining centre. The walk starts
a blast furnace and passes the
w filled-in Ashby Canal, the
mway that once carried coal
the barges, industrial hous-

ing, a pumping-engine and
lime kilns.

● Rutland Water

Virtually the entire shoreline,
24 miles long, of this magnificent reservoir can be walked.
The exception is the 350-acre
nature reserve at the western
end of the Water, which is a
major sanctuary for waterfowl.

OS maps: 128, 129, 130, 140, 141

Woolsthorpe, near Belvoir Castle.

Nottinghamshire

Suggested Walking Areas

● Clumber Park

This provides 3,000 acres of beautiful parkland, birch forest and rolling heathland.

● Cresswell Crags

Various paths run across this narrow limestone gorge, famous for its prehistoric cave dwellings.

● The Dukeries

A vast area of open heathland and forest criss-crossed by footpaths. The name refers to the old ducal estates.

● Elkesley

A 4½-mile waymarked circular walk east of Clumber Park through woodlands and fields. The going may be wet.

● Laxton

A figure of eight walk for 1½ miles through the historic village of Laxton. Laxton appeared in Domesday Book and had a motte and bailey castle. It now one of the few plac where medieval agricultu organizations can still be see including the open field s tem, enclosed paddocks a ridge and furrow cultivation.

● Papplewick and Linby

A 2½-mile circular wa through the villages of Lin and Papplewick, concentrati on the local architecture whi is mostly built in the Magnesi Limestone quarried at Lin The Trail starts at Linby, at t early medieval church of Michael, and passes the disus Castle Mill before reaching t turning-point at St Jam church in Papplewick. T going is easy but may be wet.

● Sherwood Forest

There are three waymark walks through what remains the old Forest of Sherwood now a Country Park. All sta and end at the Visitors Centr **Major Oak Path**: 1 mile gravelled footpath passi through old oak woodlan taking in the Major Oak – t forest's largest tree and Rob Hood's meeting-place. **Greenwood Walk**: nearly miles of variegated woodlan through avenues of birch a oak. **Birklands Ramble**: 3½-mi walk through the older a thicker parts of the forest.

● Stanford-on-Soar

An 8½-mile circular footpa provides very pleasant walki through fields, wooded par land and along river ban through the villages of We Leake, Sutton Bonington ar Normanton-on-Soar. The g ing may be muddy.

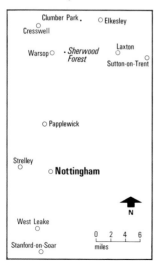

Strelley and Cossall

A 5½-mile circular walk on waymarked field paths and tracks starts in Strelley and passes the 16th-century Strelley Hall and Spring Wood before reaching Cossall. Both villages are of architectural interest.

Sutton-on-Trent

A 2½-mile circle from Sutton using the towpath by the River Trent.

Warsop

A 6-mile circular path around Warsop, mostly through lovely woodlands.

West Leake

The 4½-mile West Leake Circular Trail runs through the West Leake hills to and from the village of West Leake, which has a medieval stone church. Points of interest along the way include very good views of South Nottinghamshire, rich birdlife, and ridge and furrow farming. The going may be muddy, and some of the sections of the path are steep.

OS map: 120

Sherwood Forest.

Lincolnshire

The Viking Way

Essential Information

Length: 140 miles, from the Humber Bridge in the north to Oakham in the south

Going: gentle and easy

OS maps: 112, 113, 121, 122, 130, 141

The Viking Way runs right through Lincolnshire, having started at the south end of the Humber Bridge in Humberside and finishing across the Leicestershire border at Oakham. It owes its name to the long Scandinavian presence in the eastern counties. Parts of the waymarked path cross farmland, the rest following significant features of the landscape. Starting at the south bank of the Humber, the Way moves southwards into the beautiful Lincolnshire Wolds through the Saxon-Danish villages of Bigby, Searby and Clixby to Caistor, a Roman settlement, and on to the charming village of Tealby.

From Donington on Bain it follows the Bain valley to Goulceby and then the Waring Valley to Horncastle, the Spa Trail, a 7-mile disused railway track carrying it on to Woodhall Spa. The Witham Valley continues the Way to the cathedral city of Lincoln, from where the limestone escarpment of the Lincoln Cliff leads in turn to the valley of the Upper Witham and then along the Grantham Canal towpath and past Buckminster into Oakham by way of Rutland Water.

Suggested Walking Areas

The following are specially waymarked walks in the Lincolnshire countryside.

● Bardney

This 10-mile route around Bardney takes in the site of the Abbey, a place of worship since the 7th century, and the late medieval parish church of S Lawrence. It passes through Southrey Wood and across open fields which still show evidence of medieval strip cultivation.

● Fishtoft

A 7-mile circular walk of special Fenland character centred on Fishtoft, a small village near Boston. The route runs along the banks of Witham Haven and the Hobble drain, which carries away excess rainwater from the fenlands.

● Grimsthorpe Estate

This 15-mile walk through the Estate and Park starts in the village of Edenham, where there is a 12th-century church. In Bourne Wood there is a wide variety of trees and the lake and surrounding gardens were designed by Capability Brown. The path goes through the medieval village of Swinstead before reaching Grimsthorpe Castle, whose history goes back to the early 13th century.

Map showing Kingston-upon-Hull, Humber, Searby, Bigby, Caistor, Grimsby, Gainsborough, Tealby, Donington-on-Bain, Goulceby, Lincoln, Bardney, Horncastle, Newark-on-Trent, Temple Bruer, Woodhall Spa, Nottingham, Heckington, The Wash, Barrowby, Grantham, Fishtoft, Boston, Buckminster, Swinstead, Grimsthorpe, Kings Lynn, Edenham, Oakham, Rutland Water. Scale 0 5 10 miles. N.

Heckington Fen

On this 8-mile circle from the village of Heckington through Heckington Fen, there is evidence of Fenland history from Roman times, when they set to work to drain many of the areas, building great dykes to hold back the sea.

In Heckington village itself are the 14th-century St Andrew's Church and the Nag's Head, legendary base of the infamous Dick Turpin.

Temple Bruer

For some of the time this 8-mile circle on green tracks across the open countryside of the Lincolnshire Heath follows the Roman Ermine Street. Another place of historical interest is the 13th-century tower of the Preceptory of the Knights Templar.

Vale of Belvoir

Of particular interest to the naturalist, this 12-mile walk passes through woods and parkland and along parts of the Grantham Canal towpath; Denton Reservoir is famous for its bird-life. At Barrowby and Denton, there are Iron Age remains, and at Denton and Harlaxton Lodge there are traces of Roman occupation.

OS maps: 112, 113, 121, 122, 130, 131, 142

Lincoln Cathedral.

Cambridgeshire

Suggested Walking Areas

● Ely

The Ely Nature Trail is a 3-mile circular walk through the Isle of Ely past Roswell Pits and across water meadows by the River Ouse.

● Ely and Little Thetford

An 8½-mile circular walk from Barton Square, Ely, to Little Thetford and back.

● Grafham Water

The Savages Spinney Nature Trail runs for 3½ miles along the northern the shore of Grafham Water.

● Huntingdonshire

There are many walks through pretty country and villages:
Ramsey to Bury (5 miles)
Earith and Bluntisham (6 miles)
Upton to Sawtry and the Giddings (12 miles).

● The Nene Way

This 8-mile walk runs along the Nene Valley from the centre of Peterborough to Wansford station. Skirting the Ferry Meadows Country Park, i passes through Bluebell Wall Plantation and by two historic mills at Castor and Wate Newton. Wansford station i on the Nene Valley Railway, a private, steam-operated line.

● Wicken Fen

Footpaths cross these 730 acre of undrained fenland. A way marked 2-mile walk points ou the area's special natura features.

● The Wimpole Way

Cambridgeshire's most splen did stately home is the goal o this 11½-mile walk. Starting a Burrell's Walk in Cambridge, i runs through tree plantation to Caldecote and Kingston (ir both villages the medieva churches are worth a visit) Finally comes Wimpole Park where there is a folly and attractive gardens.

OS Maps: 131, 141, 142, 143, 153, 154

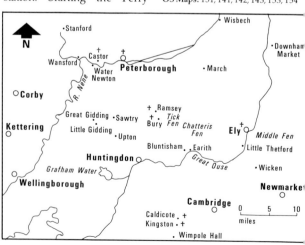

Norfolk

Suggested Walking Areas

● The Broads

Eight two-hour walks criss-cross the eastern Broads from: Horning, Dilham Staithe and Horning Lock, How Hill, Womack Water, St Benet's Abbey, Potter Heigham, Horsey, Martham.

● Hellesdon to Drayton

2½-mile footpath following the Wensum Valley with a riverside walk into Norwich.

● Norfolk Heritage Coast

There are many pleasant walks, 2-2½ hours long, between Holme-next-the-Sea and Cromer starting from: Holme Nature Reserve, Thornham Harbour, Brancaster fort, Tichwell Reserve, The Burnhams, Burnham Thorpe, Wells and Warham All Saints, Stiffkey and Cockthorpe, Blakeney, Cley and Wiveton, Kelling and Salthouse, Sheringham and Beeston Regis, East and West Runton.

● Norfolk Parish Walks

A series of circular walks on public rights of way from 3 to 6 miles long in the following parishes: Stalham; Plumstead; Salhouse; Mundesley; Aylsham, Watton; Terrington St Clements; Bradwell; North Elmham; Briston; East Dereham.

● Peddars Way

This 50-mile path runs from Knettishall to Holme largely on the route of a Roman road.

● South Norfolk Footways

A series of circular village walks between 3 and 5 miles on footpaths from Framingham Earl, Hingham, Loddon, Poringland, Wymondham.

● Weaver's Way

This 29-mile walk from Cromer to Stalham runs through the heartland of the Norfolk weaving trade, passing near Cromer, Felbrigg and Hanworth Halls. Then come two fine churches at Alby and Calthorpe before Blickling and the market towns of Aylsham and North Walsham, and the villages of Bengate, Honing, and East Ruston. The walk ends at Stalham.

OS maps: 131, 132, 133, 134, 144, 156

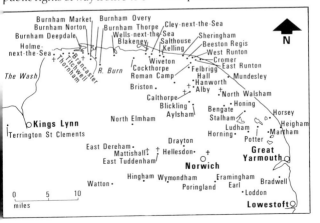

Suffolk

Suggested Walking Areas

● Gipping Valley Path

For most of its 17-mile route, this Path follows the towpath of the Ipswich–Stowmarket Navigation. The start is at the Maltings at Stowmarket. At Badley the first of several fascinating water mills is passed. A short detour brings the walker to Needham Market, well worth a visit for its pleasant buildings. Near Ipswich the scene becomes more industrial, and the conclusion is at Ipswich Docks.

● Hadleigh Railway Walk

A pleasant walk with views over the Brett Valley from Hadleigh Old Station Yard.

● The Lavenham Walk

A 4-mile path along a disused railway line from Lavenham to Long Melford.

● South-east Suffolk

In this corner of the county are many fine circular walks on footpaths and minor roads:
Stratford St Mary (7 miles) via Dedham Vale and East Bergholt
Freston and Wherstead (5 miles) with good views of the River Orwell and Ipswich Docks
The Bealings and the Fynn Valley (6 miles)
Sutton to Shottisham (5 miles) on sandy heathland tracks
Foxhall and Rushmere Heath (6 miles)
The Shotley Peninsula (6 miles) with the Orwell on one side and the Stour on the other

● Suffolk Coast Path

The Path runs for 45 miles from Bawdsey to Kessingland, occasionally deviating inland around river estuaries. There is much fine walking, with splendid sea-views along the Suffolk Heritage Coast. High-points include Aldeburgh and Southwold.

● Thornham Park

There are five waymarked walks, between ½ and 6 miles, through this pleasant park and farmland.

OS maps: 134, 143, 144, 154, 155, 156, 169

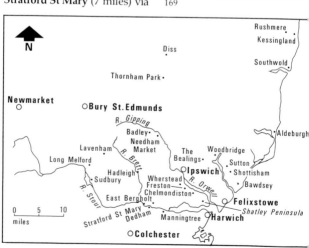

Northamptonshire

The Knightley Way

Essential Information

Length: 12 miles, from Badby to Greens Norton
Going: easy
OS map: 152

This is a delightful walk across pleasant undulating country for the most part on land once owned by the Knightley family of Fawsley Hall. Fawsley Park, crossed by the Way, was designed by Capability Brown. Other landmarks are examples of ridge and furrow farming and a handsome avenue of limes in front of Litchborough House.

The Grafton Way

Essential Information

Length: 12½ miles from Greens Norton to Wolverton (Buckinghamshire)
Going: easy
OS map: 152

This is a link path between the Knightley Way and the northern point of the North Buckinghamshire Way (see page 37). Named for the Duke of Grafton, on those land much of the Way runs, it is a pleasant walk along tracks, fieldpaths and canal towpaths.

Suggested Walking Areas

Pleasant circular family walks through the county of 'Squires and Spires' are as follows:
Oundle to Ashton (6 miles)
Thorpe Waterville to Achurch with an extension to Lilford Hall (7 miles)
Woodford to Denford (6½ miles)
Cranford circular (5½ miles) from the charming villages of Cranford St John and Cranford St Andrew
Kettering to Thorpe Malsor (6 miles) past Cransley reservoir
Earls Barton circular (3¾ miles) taking in Earls Barton church and its 10th-century tower
Delapre Abbey Gates to Wootton (6¾ miles)
Lower and Upper Harlestone circular (4 miles)
Kingsthorpe to Dallington (5 miles) through fine parkland
Linear walks include:
Great Oakley to Kettering (5½ miles) past the site of a Cistercian Abbey at Pipewell
Wilby to Little Irchester (3½ miles) overlooking the Nene Valley
Salcey Forest, 4 miles south of Wootton, and **Wakerley Wood**.
OS maps: 140, 141, 142, 151, 152, 153

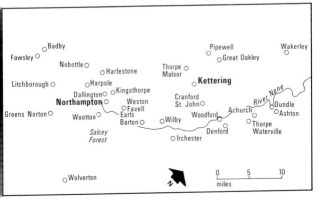

The North

Here is a grand walking land, one that, sooner or later, exerts its pull on all enthusiastic walkers. The centrepiece is indisputably the Pennine Way, a commanding route running for 250 miles up the centre of England, from the Peak District, through the moors of West Yorkshire and the Yorkshire Dales into Teesdale and on to the Northumberland forests and the Cheviots, terminating at Kirk Yetholm on the Scottish border. As befits the first long-distance path established, this is the finest and most challenging of all of them. In many stretches the going is hard, and walkers must draw on all their reserves: but the effort is more than rewarded.

The attractions of the rest of the region are innumerable. There are two other long-distance paths. The Cleveland Way is the more varied and demanding, running across a wild and isolated stretch of the North York Moors and then along the North Sea coast. The Wolds Way is a

1   Merseyside
2   Cheshire
3   Derbyshire
4   Greater Manchester
5   Lancashire
6   West Yorkshire
7   South Yorkshire
8   Humberside
9   North Yorkshire
10 Cumbria
11 Durham
12 Cleveland
13 Tyne and Wear
14 Northumberland

gentler route through the rolling Yorkshire Wolds, some of England's richest agricultural country.

But in the opinion of many these two routes are overshadowed by the splendour of the Lake District, the Dales, the Moors – indeed by virtually every part of the region. The Lake District is as good a country for walkers as it is for climbers, and there are magnificent low- and middle-level routes. The North York Moors are tough, high and challenging, the Dales softer but just as stimulating. Elsewhere, there is fine walking too: in the Peak District, in Lancashire's Forest of Bowland, on the Durham moors, along Hadrian's Wall and through the Northumberland National Park.

The north is indeed a mecca for walkers.

Practical Points on Moorland Walking

● Proficiency with map and compass is essential, as visibility is often restricted.

● When embarking on a trek over a three-day week-end, keep the mileage on the second day modest. Moorland walking saps stamina, especially after heavy rain.

● Despite good waterproofs and high-quality boots, you will invariably be wet by the end of the day. Dry clothing and socks can do wonders for the morale.

● Peat puddles have a high acidic content so be sure to dowse boots with fresh water to prevent the leather from rotting.

● Put on waterproofs to offset the chill on windy tops. Wear sunglasses against the worst of peat dust which is often stirred up in dry, windy conditions.

● When planning an expedition remember the trusted formula which decrees one hour for every three miles on the map, plus one hour more for every 2000 feet of altitude.

The Pennine Way

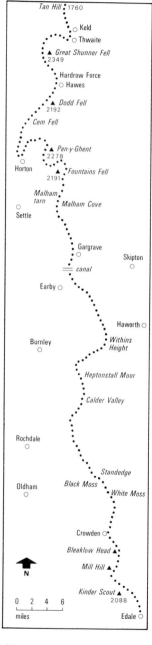

Tan Hill • 1760
○ Keld
○ Thwaite
▲ Great Shunner Fell
2349
Hardrow Force
○ Hawes
▲ Dodd Fell
2192
Cem Fell
▲ Pen-y-Ghent
2278
○ Horton
▲ Fountains Fell
2191
Malham tarn
○ Settle
Malham Cove
Gargrave ○
Skipton ○
══ canal
Earby ○
Haworth ○
Burnley ○
Withins Height
Heptonstall Moor
Calder Valley
Rochdale ○
Standedge
Oldham ○
Black Moss
White Moss
Crowden ○
Bleaklow Head ▲
Mill Hill ▲
Kinder Scout ▲
2088
Edale ○

N

0 2 4 6
miles

Essential Information

Length: 251 miles, from Edale in the Derbyshire Peak District to Kirk Yetholm on the Scottish border
Going: very difficult with numerous tough ascents
Terrain: principally mountains, fells and moorland
OS maps: 74, 80, 86, 87, 91, 92, 98, 103 109, 110

Although not the longest of Britain's long-distance paths, the Pennine Way is certainly the most challenging. Even the most experienced walker will prepare carefully for this path along the backbone of England, from the Peak District north to the Yorkshire Dales, Teesdale and the moorland and forests of Northumberland. Protective clothing and map and compass are absolute essentials. And walkers must keep a careful watch on the weather, which is unreliable and changeable.

Edale to Haworth: 49 miles

Dominated by the towering mass of Kinder Scout, Edale makes a fitting beginning to the Way. The path starts as it goes on, with a sharp climb up Grindsbrook and Kinder Scout. Some scrambling is needed to reach the top, and then the walker is face to face with a wide expanse of moorland, which may seem firm but is usually wet and sludgy. The target is Kinder Downfall along an ill-defined path, then Black Ashop Moor, Mill Hill, Bleaklow Head and Torside Clough. All this is hard going, though there are some fine views in compensation. The descent to Crowden is relatively easy, but then there is another climb to Wessenden Moor, White Moss and Black Moss. A short respite through Standedge precedes a

...inder Downfall.

entler walk (by Pennine Way standards) through the Calder Valley and across Heptonstall Moor to High Withins. Haworth, where the Brontë Museum is worth a visit, is 3 miles to the east.

Haworth to Hawes: 57 miles

From here the scenery slowly changes, the peat moors falling back and giving way to the gentler, less foreboding Dales. The stretch to Gargrave is relatively easy, with a pleasant section along the towpath of the Leeds and Liverpool Canal. Then it is over Eshton Moor to Malham Dale, green and fertile, past the spectacular Malham Cove and up to Malham Tarn. Two summits follow, Foun-

tains Fell and Pen-y-Ghent, one of Yorkshire's Three Peaks (see page 133), and then the Way falls to Horton, only to climb again to cross Cam Fell and Dodd Fell. Finally it comes to Hawes, home of the celebrated sheep market and a delightful town with winding streets.

Hawes to Dufton: 51 miles

After Hardrow Force, there is a sharp climb up Great Shunner Fell on a well-defined path. Then come Thwaite and Keld, both charming stone-built villages, and the ascent of Tan Hill, where a welcoming pub awaits walkers on the summit. Now there is a really tough 20-mile trek across moorland

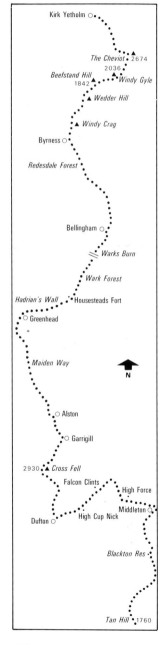

The Way above Dufton.

to Middleton - in - Teesdale, desolate walk that takes a lon day. An alternative path run into Bowes and rejoins th Way at Blackton reservoir. Th next targets are the falls at Lo Force and High Force on th Tees and then Falcon Clint The walk into Dufton pa High Cup Nick is magnificer and the views are stunnin; this is certainly one of the be moments in the entire 25 miles.

Dufton to Housesteads: 43 miles

Knock Fell, Great Dun Fell an Cross Fell, the highest on th entire Pennine Way, com next, before a sharp descent t Garrigill and Alston, an attrac tive market town. Though turn now to the Roman occu pation of Britain and to th soldiers whose unpleasant jo it was to guard the norther rim of the great Roman Empir from invasion. First the Wa runs along Maiden Way, Roman road, and then, afte Hartleyburn and Blenkinsop Commons, it meets Hadrian Wall at Greenhead. There is a 8-mile stretch along the Wa itself to Housesteads. This i

Malham Cove.

perhaps the best Wall walk, and there is much of interest, including the fort at House-steads, the only one fully exca-ated, and a museum.

Housesteads to Kirk Yetholm: 1 miles

North from Housesteads, into Wark Forest, the path is hard going and the surroundings sombre. Then it crosses Wark urn and follows the North Tyne Valley to Bellingham, the last place of any size along the Way. The last haul is also the longest – 39 miles through the Cheviots with only one tiny village, Byrness, along the path. Beyond Redesdale Forest, there is a series of summits – Windy Crag, Ogre Hill, Wedder Hill, Beefstand Hill, and finally The Cheviot itself, 2,675 feet up – before the last descent to Kirk Yetholm.

111

The Cleveland Way

Essential Information

Length: 110 miles, from Helmsley north and north-east to the coast at Saltburn, then south to Filey
Going: hard, very hard occasionally
Terrain: high moorland and seaside cliffs with frequent ups and downs
OS maps: 86, 93, 94, 101

The Cleveland Way is a challenge for the experienced walker. The less experienced should tackle it with extreme caution. The vagaries of the weather should always be respected. But the wild scenery, and continual historical, natural and geological interest, give walkers a rewarding trek across the North York Moors and along the east coast.

Helmsley to Osmotherley: 26 miles

The Way begins in Helmsley Market Square. But before starting visit Rievaulx Abbey founded in 1131 by Cistercian monks. From the town the path climbs steeply through woods and forest through Nestle Dale and Flassen Dale, and up to the moor at Cold Kirby. There are woods behind, the moorland stretches ahead. There is a good walk to Sutton Bank, a fine scarp with views of Gibbon Lake continuing over Hambleton Ridge, where there is a National Park Information Centre. From the ridge the Vale of York is a fine sight; look out for the lime-covered White Horse with Kilburn below. Along Sutton Brow, north across Whitestone Cliffs, where caution is needed as there are some nasty drops, the Hambleton Hills take the Way to Osmotherley. It is heavy going across the moors, bracing walking and good open views.

Osmotherley to Guisborough: 26 miles

Shortly after leaving Osmotherley the Cleveland Way follows the Lyke Wake Walk, the tough 40-mile trek across the moors (see page 130) for about 12 miles. The stretch to Broughton provides desolate landscapes and high panoramic views, gradually rising to Urra Moor, the highest point of the walk (1,500 feet). Leaving the Lyke Wake the path goes down to Kildale. The woods here are a welcome break from the moorlands above. Back on

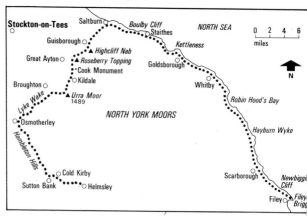

Easby Moor, there is a two-route option, the easier one passing along Coate Moor via a memorial to Captain Cook and on to Great Ayton. The track of the main route should only be used in fine weather. Either route takes the path north, then east of the 1,000-foot peak of Roseberry Topping, to Highcliff Nab and Guisborough.

Guisborough to Robin Hood's Bay: 36 miles

There is undulating country to Saltburn and the North Sea coast. Here the tides should be respected and the cliff walk needs care. The challenging conditions are worth tackling as the sea views are very fine, especially at the 600-foot Boulby cliff. The fishing village of Staithes is the next objective, where a rest refreshes the

Robin Hood's Bay.

walker for the section to Whitby, 12 miles ahead. The cliff walk continues with Kettleness Headland, the Roman fort near Goldsborough and very fine scenery to the port at Whitby. This lovely fishing town, with the Sailors' Church, museum and fine Abbey, makes a welcome break before the 8 miles to Robin Hood's Bay.

Robin Hood's Bay to Filey: 22 miles

The coastal stretch continues with steep inclines along the cliff edge, past the cove at Hayburn Wyke to the busy resort of Scarborough.

The last 8 miles are an easy walk and less isolated than the preceding stretches. The end is gentle, Filey Brigg giving a suitable climax to the walk with superb views of Filey town and Flamborough Head.

The Wolds Way

Essential Information

Length: 81 miles, from Hessle (Humberside) to Filey (North Yorkshire)
Going: mostly easy, with a few stiffish climbs
Terrain: chiefly rich farmland, with chalk downland in the Wolds
OS maps: 100, 101, 106

The Wolds Way runs through some of Britain's most fertile and beautiful countryside. Unlike the other long-distance paths, it is a relatively easy walk and can be happily tackled by even the most inexperienced walker: it presents no major physical challenges. And, spared gruelling switchbacks and stamina-testing stretches, walkers have more time – and energy – to enjoy the splendour of the scenery.

Hessle to Goodmanham: 24 miles

The Way starts on the north bank of the Humber, at the Ferry Boat Inn by Hessle Haven and a short walk from the north end of the Humber Bridge. This is a good spot for enthusiastic walkers: the East Riding Heritage Way starts the same place, the Hull Countryway passes through and, from the southern bank of the Humber, the Viking Way moves off through Lincolnshire to Oakham (see page 100).

The Way runs along the foreshore to North Ferriby and then turns inland to run through woods and past a quarry to Welton. At an inn here – the Green Man – Dick Turpin is said to have been arrested in 1739. Now the path takes the walker through Welton Dale, on to Brantingham and then through Ellerker, North Wood to the edge of South Cave. This is true Wolds country now, wooded and well cultivated. There now follows an 11-mile stretch to Goodmanham through Little Wold Plantation, along a disused railway track for a short way, up through Hunsley Dale to Swindale and Newbald Wood and across the Beverley to York road. A link path runs into

Map showing the Wolds Way route with locations including: Muston, Folkton, Filey, Sherburn, Staxton, Wintringham, Settrington, Wharram, Thixendale, Fridaythorpe, Huggate, Nettle Dale, Millington, Nunburnholme, Londesborough, Goodmanham, Market Weighton, Newbald Wood, South Cave, Welton, N. Ferriby, Hessle, Humber bridge, Hull. Scale: 0 2 4 6 miles. THE WOLDS. N (north arrow).

Humber Bridge.

The Wolds.

Market Weighton along another old railway from Rifle Butts Quarry just before Goodmanham.

Goodmanham to Thixendale: 20 miles

From Goodmanham the Way makes for the Londesborough Estate along the course of a Roman road that ran from Malton to Brough. The park was landscaped by the Dukes of Devonshire, who had a seat here until the early 19th century. Past Londesborough Hall the target is Nunburnholme, named after a Benedictine nunnery of which no trace remains, and then Warrendale (there are views across to York and the Minster here) and past Millington Pastures. Until the 1960s, when the area was enclosed and ploughed up, this was sheep-grazing land much as it had been in the Middle Ages. From the bottom of Rabbit Warren there is a steep climb up and then down again into Nettle Dale. Then it is a short walk along the Huggate Sheepwalk into Huggate, one of the highest villages in the Wolds. Fridaythorpe is the next village, from where a beautiful stretch of the Way leads to Thixendale.

Thixendale to Filey: 37 miles

This is the remotest part of the walk, a quiet and peaceful country. Past North Plantation, the Way makes for Wharram le Street. The short detour to Wharram Percy is well worthwhile. The village was a thriving community in the Middle Ages, but the Black Death wiped out the residents in about 1350, and habitation ceased entirely in the early 16th century. Running beside Cinquefoil Hill, the Way passes Settrington High Barn and Beacon Wold to reach one of the most impressive views in the whole walk, across the flat farmland of the Vale of Pickering and towards the North York Moors. Now comes Wintringham and then Sherburn and Ganton. From here the path runs past RAF Staxton Wold, then climbs back up the escarpment, round Folkton Wold and then down again to Muston. From here it is a short walk into Filey. The Way ends north of the town at Newbiggin Cliff, a little beyond Filey Brigg. This is also the end-point of the Cleveland Way (see pages 112-113).

115

Merseyside

The Wirrall Way

Essential Information

Length: 12 miles, from West Kirby to Hooton (Cheshire)
Going: easy, but often wet and muddy
OS maps: 108, 117

This is a railway walk, along the track of the old West Kirby to Hooton line. The start is from the site of West Kirby station, and almost immediately the Way heads towards the Dee estuary. Then it runs alongside Caldy golf course before cuttings bring it to Thurstaston. Parkgate is the next target, with good views of the estuary *en route*, followed by Neston and a spectacular sandstone cutting. The line turns inland now to Willaston and Hooton.

Suggested Walking Areas

● Calderstones Park

The mansion in Calderstones Park is the starting-point for a 1¼-mile trail across the park.

● Caldy

The Dee foreshore can be followed from Caldy to Thurstaston. But beware the tides, which sometimes come right up to the cliff bottom.

● Eastham Woods

The Eastham Woods Trail is a 1-mile walk through Eastham Woods, covering the Mersey estuary, woodland and local history.

● Neston

At the end of Old Quay Lane a short path runs to the Old Quay, whose heyday was in about 1600, and on to Wirral Colliery, opened in 1750, and Denhall Quay.

● North Wirral

The North Wirral Coastal Park runs along the coast for 5 miles from New Brighton to Meols Parade.

● Thurstaston

The Thurstaston Nature Trail runs for 1 mile through the Wirral Country Park from the visitor centre. A short footpath also leads from Thurstaston village up the hill from where there are magnificent views.

OS maps: 108, 117

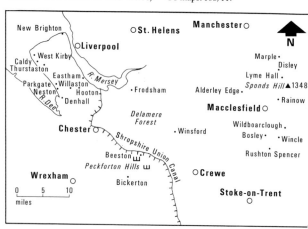

Cheshire

Macclesfield.

Part of the Wirral Way (see page 116) runs through the county.

The Gritstone Trail

Essential Information

Length: 18½ miles, from Lyme Park, south of Higher Disley, to Rushton
Going: fairly easy, with some hill climbs
OS maps: 109, 118

Gritstone dominates the Cheshire hills, giving the area its particular character and this Trail its name. The path winds through fine country with constant views of the Peak District to the east. The start is at Lyme Hall, and the Trail runs through the Park and out on to moorland, uphill to Sponds Hill, then follows an ancient ridge track. Past Brink Farm the walker reaches Andrew's Knob, an abandoned stone quarry. Then comes the descent to the Cheshire Hunt Inn, Ingersley Clough and a climb up Kerridge Hill, topped by White Nancy, a folly built in about 1820.

Now there are good views as the path descends to Rainow, climbs Gorsey Brow and then crosses fields to Windyway Head (8 miles). After Tegg's Nose, the next target is the Hill of Rossenclowes, reached after some valley walking, and then Croker Hill, itself 1,286 feet but surmounted by a Post Office tower another 286 feet high. It is downhill again now, then up and along the crest of the Minns, known as Bosley Minn on the west side and Wincle Minn on the east. There are splendid views now, Mow Cop and the Cloud standing lonely and prominent. The last stretch crosses Barleyford Bridge to Rushton, which is also the start of the Staffordshire Way (see page 94).

The Sandstone Trail

Essential Information

Length: 30 miles, from Beacon Hill, Frodsham, to Grindley Brook locks
Going: easy, but some stiff climbs
OS map: 117

This Trail follows the Central Cheshire Ridge, sandstone hills that run practically the length of Cheshire. To the north of the start at Beacon Hill lie the factories and chemical works gathered round the Mersey. But walkers turn their backs on this, face south and

117

Beeston Castle.

descends Dunsdale Hollow. Climbing up again, the Trail passes Woodhouse Hill Fort, which dates from the Iron Age, crosses Snidley Moor and makes for Simmonds Hill and Manley. Delamere Forest, the next objective, is a tiny part of the huge forest that once covered much of Cheshire. Then come Nettlefold and Primrose Hill Woods, Willington Wood and Wood Lane.

Striking along Old Gypsy Lane, a green lane, the walker now enters dairy cattle country – Cheshire is one of the biggest milk-producers in the UK – crosses the Shropshire Union Canal at Wharton's Lock and drops to the River Gowy (13½ miles). Beeston Crag, topped by a ruined castle, precedes Peckforton Wood and a pleasant stretch along the Peckforton Hills. Next Bulkeley Hill is climbed, and then comes Rawhead, the highest spot on the walk (746 feet), Tower Wood, Bickerton, Maiden Castle, an Iron Age camp, and Hether Wood. Now the hills are left behind, and it is plain

walking to Hampton Green, Bickleywood and the Shropshire Union Canal at Willeymoor Lock. The final stretch is along the towpath to Grindley Brook.

Suggested Walking Areas

● Alderley Edge

There is fine walking along the 600-foot sandstone ridge and its wooded slopes.

● Beeston

Two castles – one the remains of a medieval stronghold, the other a 19th century re-creation – can be reached in a pleasant 3½-mile walk from Beeston. The path runs up to the foot of Beeston Castle, across the plain to the Peckforton Hills and around the wooded slopes on which Peckforton Castle stands.

● Macclesfield

There are good walks through Macclesfield Forest and on the open moorland nearby. One worthwhile path runs from Langley through the Forest and across the northern side of Shutlingsloe, one of the most prominent hills in the area, to Wildboarclough, said to be the place where the last wild boar in England was killed.

● Marple

There are pleasant, wooded footpaths from the town, which clings to the banks of the River Goyt, along the river bank and up on to moorland.

● Winsford

The Whitegate Way is a 6-mile path along the now disused line from Winsford Junction to Catsclough.

OS maps: 109, 117, 118

Derbyshire

The Pennine Way starts at Edale below Kinder Scout in the Dark Peak (see page 108). The first miles are a tough walk, but a rewarding one.

High Peak Trail

Essential Information

Length: 17½ miles, from Cromford to Dowlow, near Buxton
Going: easy
OS map: 119

This Trail follows the route of the Cromford and High Peak railway, opened in 1830 as a link route between the Cromford and the Peak Forest Canals. There is superb scenery throughout, in both the Derwent Valley and on the unspoilt Peak District uplands.

The start is at the junction of the railway and the Cromford Canal. Cromford wharf and the Leawood pump house are passed on the way to the Sheep Pasture incline, where the gradient is between 1 in 8 and 1

in 9. An engine-house at the top contained the winding engines. The path leads on to the Middleton incline and its engine-house and then makes for Hopton tunnel, 113 yards long, and Hopton incline. Past Longcliffe station the Trail moves on to the open uplands, meeting the Tissington Trail (see below) at Parsley Hay, and runs through Hurdlow to Dowlow.

The Tissington Trail

Essential Information

Length: 13 miles, from Ashbourne to Parsley Hay
Going: easy
OS map: 119

Also a railway route, on the old Ashbourne to Buxton line, this path runs south/north through the county. The start is at Ashbourne, a fine old Georgian town, and then the Trail meanders north through Thorpe, Tissington itself, Alsop en le Dale to Hartington. Near Hartington there are good views over the Dove Valley. The final 1½ miles bring the walker to the junction with the High Peak Trail.

The Monsal Trail

Essential Information

Length: 8 miles, plus link footpaths, from Blackwell Mill Cottages, 3 miles east of Buxton, to Coombs Viaduct, 1 mile south-east of Bakewell
Going: easy on the main path but quite difficult on the link routes
OS map: 119

The former Midland line is the route for this trail, which runs through limestone country, advertised by the railway company when the line was opened as 'Little Switzerland'. The Trail is divided into four parts,

separated by tunnels. These are not open to the public, and paths round them must be followed. From Blackwell Mill Cottages there is a 1-mile walk through Chee Dale to the first tunnel, then a 2-mile section through Millers Dale to Litton Dale, followed by yet another tunnel, and then a 1-mile stretch to Monsal Head. The last tunnel precedes the longest part of the path, 4 miles to the Coombs Road Viaduct. There are plans to reopen railway traffic on the line, and if that happens footpath and railway will run next to each other, separated by a fence.

Suggested Walking Areas

● Arbor Low

A 1-mile walk leads from the A515 up to this magnificent ancient stone circle, one of the largest in northern England. On nearby Gib Hill a Bronze Age tumulus stands on a Neolithic cairn. The site also makes an interesting diversion from the Lathkill Dale walk. Turn up Cales Dale past Cales Farm to Long Rake, cross the minor road and walk up to the summit.

Dovedale.

● Bradford Dale

This dale, a little to the south of Lathkill Dale, is among the most beautiful in Derbyshire. It runs from Dale End, near Elton, to Alport. The stretch between Middleton-by-Youlgreave and Alport is especially recommended.

● Buxton

This elegant spa town is the starting-point for a fairly rigorous 7½-mile walk past Solomon's Temple (a tower built by an inn-keeper named Solomon) over Diamond Hill to Dalehead. The route continues over Chrome Hill to Nab End and the end of the walk at Longton.

● Derby

There is an enjoyable 8-mile walk from Boulton Lane, on the outskirts of the town, across Sinfin Moor to Barrow-on-Trent and Swarkestone, returning to Shelton Lock.

● Dovedale

Start the walk north up the Dale from the twenty Stepping Stones near Thorpe. Immediately there is a series of amazing rock formations, among them Bunster, Thorpe Cloud and the Twelve Apostles. Tissington Spires leads to Reynard's Kitchen, a hillside cave reached through a natural limestone arch. The path narrows at The Straits, opens out a little later before Milldale and then continues upstream to Wolfscote Dale and the wooded Beresford Dale. The final leg of the path takes the walker into Hartington.

● Duffield

A pleasant 4-mile walk leads

River Dove, Dovedale.

om the Chevin golf house utside Duffield through azelwood and over Sunny ank to Milford.

Edale

here is a good deal of hard oing on the 12-mile route orth-west from Edale to Hayeld and Chisworth. From dale the first target is Roych lough. Then comes Mount amine and the path into Hayeld. The next section, from which there are good views of inder Scout, runs alongside antern Pike, over Matley Moor and Far Cown Edge and hence into Chisworth.

Errwood Reservoir

4-mile circular walk leads om Errwood Reservoir along Roman road called The Street Foxlow Edge and the ruins f Errwood Hall.

Grindleford

he Derwent and Wye Valleys re connected by a 7½-mile oute from Grindleford station hrough Froggatt and Stoney Middleton. Then comes a timulating stretch across Longstone Moor into Great Longstone, from where it is just a short walk to Monsal Head.

● Lathkill Dale

Downstream from Monyash, the dale starts spectacularly with limestone crags, becoming more wooded as it descends, past Mandale mine, where the former engine house can be seen, to Over Haddon and Alport.

● Mam Tor

A 4½-mile circular route runs from Castleton to Hollins Cross and the top of Mam Tor, returning via Windy Knoll and Winnats Pass.

● Sett Valley Trail

This Trail runs for 2½ miles along an old railway line from New Mills to Hayfield. The Sett Valley was a major textile centre in the 18th century, and some of the weavers' houses, with weaving rooms on the top floor, still stand.

OS maps: 110, 119, 120, 128, 129

South Yorkshire

The Cal-der-went Walk

Essential Information

Length: 30 miles, from the River Calder at Horbury Bridge, Wakefield southwest to the River Derwent at Ladybower Reservoir (Derbyshire)
Going: varied, with easy and fairly tough stretches
OS map: 110

This path links the two rivers of its title: the Calder and the Derwent. The route runs along the Dearne, Don and Porter Valleys near some of the county's industrial heartland. The conclusion is just over the Derbyshire border, in the Peak District National Park.

Suggested Walking Areas

● The Cannon Hall Walk

This 5-mile circular route runs through the Cannon Hall Country Park on the south-eastern slopes of the Pennines. It starts at the car park near Cascade Bridge, and runs through Cawthorne, Margery Wood and High Hoyland, pa Cannon Hall to Winter Hill.

● Ewden Valley

Several footpaths run alor Ewden Beck past reservoirs the moorlands.

● Millstone Edge

The Millstone Edge escarp ment lies on the border wit Derbyshire. Footpaths ru from view-points on the scar over the open moorland.

● Stanage Edge

There is a good path round th rocky outcrop in the moo lands of the Peak District. Th route continues along th Roman road, known as th Long Causeway, to Redmire reservoir on Hallam Moors.

● Wharncliffe Park

There are good walks throug parkland near Deepcar up t Wharncliffe Crags, with breath taking views over the Do Valley.

OS maps: 110, 111, 112, 119, 120

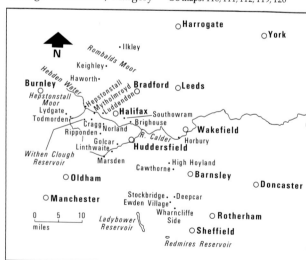

West Yorkshire

The Pennine Way runs in the west of the county (see pages 108-111). There are especially fine stretches across Blackstone Edge and Heptonstall Moor. The last stretch of the Ebor Way also runs through the county (see page 128).

The Calderdale Way

Essential Information

Length: 50 miles, in a circular route round Calderdale, from Brighouse in the east to Todmorden in the west.
Going: generally fairly easy, with some difficult stretches.
OS maps: 103, 104, 110

This is a bracing, hilly walk round Calderdale with a stimulating mixture of open country and industrial landscape. Starting from Brighouse, the Way runs along the Calder and Hebble Navigation Canal, then strikes north-west to Southowram, a hilltop village with good views of the Calder Valley. Then comes the descent to West Vale, a woodland stretch to Norland Moor and another descent, this time to Ripponden. Now it is uphill again to Flints and Slate Delf Hill, where there are good views, and down once more to Cragg. Then the walker crosses so-called 'Coiners' Country' where in the 18th century a group of counterfeiters is said to have lived, to Withens Clough Reservoir, Mankinholes and Todmorden, which is visited in two parts, with a moorland stretch between. This is an attractive town, founded on the cotton industry, not on wool as elsewhere in Yorkshire. The next objectives are Blackshaw Head and Heptonstall, once a centre of handloom-weaving.

Then there is more hill-walking to Luddenden Dean, followed by farmland through the Shibden Valley to Stone Chair and Norwood Green. The final stretch back to Brighouse, although more industrial than the rest of the Way, nevertheless remains pleasant and peaceful.

Link paths run between virtually all the towns and villages in the Calder Valley and the Calderdale Way, making access easy at many points. These paths start near Southowram and at Copley, Sowerby Bridge, Luddenden Foot, Mytholm-

Haworth.

The village of Golcar, near Huddersfield.

royd, Hebden Bridge, Sandbed, Eastwood, Lobb Mill and Todmorden.

Colne Valley Circular Walk

Essential Information

Length: 12¼ miles, in a circular route around the Colne Valley from Golcar in the north-east to Marsden in the south-west

Going: variable, with some easy sections and some fairly tough ones

OS map: 110

This circular route takes the walker right round Colne Valley through attractive country and pleasant villages. The start is at the Colne Valley Museum at Golcar. The first objective is Linthwaite, reached along the towpath of a now-disused canal

past the 'Titanic' Mills, so called because they were completed soon after the liner sank. The route on from Linthwaite to Marsden runs on minor road and field paths past Linthwaite Hall. The next stretch is more difficult, with some uphill walking and a long stretch over moorland, but excellent views in compensation. From Wiberlee it is a simple walk across fields and past Camping Wood to Golcar.

Suggested Walking Areas

● Brontë Country

From Haworth, a bleak moorland village with a Brontë Museum, there is a 3-mile walk to Brontë Falls and High Withins, said to be the setting for *Wuthering Heights.*

● Heptonstall

The **Slurring Rock Nature Trail** starts at Horse Bridge Lock on the Rochdale Canal and runs down to Hebden Water.

● Ilkley

From Ilkley there is a good 3 mile walk on the Moor to White Wells and Hangingstone Quarries, returning past the Cow and Calf Rocks and the tarn.

● Lydgate

From Lydgate a 3½-mile walk leads to Blackstone Edge and Blackstone Edge reservoir. The path runs up the Roman road from Manchester to Ilkley to Blackstone Edge, then follows Broad Head Drain to the reservoir and returns along Blackstone Edge Old Road, built in the 18th century as a trans-Pennine coaching road.

OS maps: 103, 104, 105, 109, 110, 111

Humberside

The East Riding Heritage Way

Essential Information

Length: 84 miles, from Hessle to Filey, North Yorkshire
Going: easy, except around the north side of Flamborough Head
OS maps: 101, 105, 106, 107

This is a pleasant undulating walk with only one difficult section, at Flamborough Head. The Way is divided into four sections, best known by their individual names.

The Beverley '20': Humber Bridge to Beverley: 20 miles

The Way begins at the north end of the Humber Bridge, just outside Hessle. (The Wolds Way starts here too; see page 114.) It follows the foreshore past North Ferriby, cuts inland to Welton and climbs the eastern edge of the Yorkshire Wolds near Brantingham. Then it is pleasant walking to Skidby, Walkington and Beverley. The Minster dominates the skyline from afar.

The Hutton Hike: Beverley to Driffield Riverhead: 23 miles

The Way strikes north-east. Soon there are alternative routes along the flood bank of the River Hull or Barmston Drain. Choose the river path even though it is a little longer. At Scurf Dike turn left to Cranswick and Hutton, from where it is a short walk to Driffield Riverhead.

Chalk cliffs, Thornwick Bay.

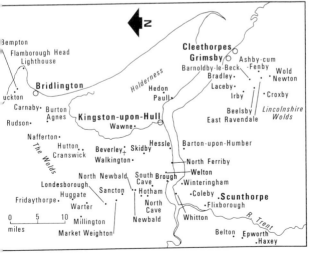

THE NORTH

HUMBERSIDE

The Hudston Roam: Driffield Riverhead to Bridlington: 21 miles

The Path follows the river again for a short way, then turns north to Nafferton and north-east to Burton Agnes. A huge dog-leg through Rudston follows the Roman road from Bridlington to York for nearly 2 miles. Finally a bridleway past Carnaby Temple, a brick folly, brings the walker to Bridlington.

The Headland Walk: Bridlington to Filey: 20 miles

This last stretch is the most exhilarating of all. The south side of the Headland is easy going, but the north, especially between Thornwick and Bempton, is only for the sure-footed. The Walk reaches the Lighthouse via Beacon Hill and South Landing, one of the two old harbours on the headland. Then come North Landing, Thornwick and the celebrated Bempton Cliffs, a bird-watcher's paradise. From Buckton it is a simple walk along the cliff tops into Filey, the end point of the Cleveland Way (see page 113).

The Hull Countryway

Essential Information

Length: 50 miles, from Hull to Paull
Going: easy
OS map: 107

This 50-mile path takes walkers along footpaths and minor roads in a large loop round Hull. The first 13 miles are along the river from the town centre through Hessle to Brough Haven. Then the Way turns inland, skirting the Wolds, to Skidby and Beverley (15 miles). Heading south-east,

the path passes Wawne an enters Holderness, an area o wide skies and long view Before Hedon (14 miles) th route is not clear and carefu map-reading is necessary. Th last section runs down to th estuary at Paull, where the ol lighthouse, built in 1836, i worth a look, and then back t Hedon again (8 miles) by different route.

Suggested Walking Areas

North Humberside

There is much good walking here, with some stiffish climb on the Yorkshire Wolds and attractive country everywhere As well as the East Riding Herit age Way, the Wolds Way run from Hessle to Filey, and the Minster Way links the two minsters at Beverley and York (see pages 125 and 114).

South Humberside

This is not a dramatic land scape, but attractive villages wide skies and, in the Lincoln shire Wolds, pleasantly undu lating land make for enjoyable easy walking. The Viking Way which runs through Lincoln shire to Oakham, starts at Barton Waterside, the southern end of the Humber Bridge (see page 100).

● Isle of Axholme

A few miles east of Doncaster, the Isle of Axholme is an in triguingly remote area. Drained as late as the 17th century, it had been marsh for centuries. Walks start from Epworth (where John Wesley and his brother Charles were born), Haxey, Woodhouse and from the picnic site between Belton and Epworth. Most are 3 to 4 miles long.

Lincolnshire Wolds

Within easy reach of Grimsby is a pleasant group of circular walks on the eastern slope of the Wolds.
Laceby to Irby and back (5 miles)
Irby Dales (7 miles); starts at Irby
Bradley Woods (10 miles); starts picnic site, Bradley Woods
Beelsby to Croxby (6 miles)
Ashby Hill (8 miles); starts Barnoldby-le-Beck
Ravensdale Wolds (8 miles); starts East Ravensdale
Hawerby Wold (6 miles); starts Wold Newton.

Millington and Huggate

Further north, the high wolds offer delightful walks with splendid views. Especially recommended are:
Millington Wolds (4 miles); starts Millington
Warter Wold (8 miles); starts Warter
Huggate Wold (10 miles or 3 walks of 4 miles); starts Huggate
Fridaythorpe Wold (6 miles); starts Fridaythorpe.

North Landing, Flamborough.

● River Trent

A path follows the Trent and Humber from the northern edge of Scunthorpe through Flixborough and Burton-upon-Stather to Alkborough, Whitton and Winteringham. Circular walks in the same area are:
Flixborough to Normanby and **Burton-upon-Stather (4 miles)**
Burton-upon-Stather to Coleby (4½ miles)
Winteringham to Whitton (5½ miles)

● The southern Yorkshire Wolds

There are many pleasant walks at the southern tip of the Yorkshire Wolds, and among the best are:
Brantingham Dale (3½ miles); starts Brantingham
Welton Wold (4 miles); starts Welton
Elloughton Wold (4 miles); starts Brantingham
Wauldby Green (4 miles); starts Wauldby
South Cave to Drewton (6½ miles)
North Cave to Hotham (6 miles)
Newbald Wolds (8 miles); starts Newbald
OS maps: 101, 106, 107, 112, 113

North Yorkshire

The Pennine Way, the Wolds Way and the Cleveland Way (see pages 108-115) all run through the county, which has good claim to be one of England's best walking areas.

The Ebor Way

Essential Information

Length: 70 miles, from Helmsley to Ilkley
Going: fairly easy
OS maps: 100, 104, 105

This is a pleasant walk through delightful country from Helmsley, starting-point also of the Cleveland Way, to Ilkley via York. From the handsome market town of Helmsley, the first target is Hovingham, reached via Oswaldkirk and Cawton. Between Cawton and Hovingham the path passes Spa House, in the 18th century a source of spa waters. The next

stretch to Strensall is through rolling farm- and woodland, a peaceful, fertile part of England. Landmarks are Terrington and Sheriff Hutton, where there are the remains of an impressive 14th-century castle. Now there is a riverside walk towards Haxby, along an overgrown path, a diversion from before Haxby to Huntington and then a river walk again into the centre of York (27 miles).

Leaving York, the Way heads for Bishopthorpe, where the Archbishop of York has his palace, then Copmanthorpe and Tadcaster. Before Tadcaster there are two stretches along the Roman road from York to Tadcaster. Now it is along the river through Newton Kyme to Boston Spa and then on field paths and tracks to Wetherby. More woodland and fields bring the walker to Harewood, where a pause to view Harewood House is essential. Then the Way makes for Bramhope and The Chevin, a huge outcrop of stone with majestic views. The final section is from Menston to Ilkley past the Cow and Calf Rocks.

The Foss Walk

Essential Information

Length: 28 miles, from York to Easingwold
Going: easy
OS maps: 100, 105

The River Foss is the backdrop for this easy-going walk, and the path follows its banks for most of the way. From York the walker heads north to New Earswick, Huntington, Old Earswick and Haxby. At Strensall the New Bridge is passed, nicknamed 'Old Humpy'. Now the objective is Cornborough, past the remains of the Foss

York Minster.

Navigation canal basin, last used in 1852, and then Farington and Marton. A diversion to Sheriff Hutton is possible from just before the canal basin. After Crayke the walker reaches Pond Head, the source of the Foss, and then it is a 5-mile walk into Easingwold, a pleasant market town.

The Esk Valley Walk

Essential Information

Length: 33 miles, from Farndale Moor to Whitby
Going: easy, with some slightly more difficult hill and moorland stretches
OS maps: 94, 100, 101

This walk across the North York Moors National Path runs along the Esk Valley, beside the Esk Valley Railway. The start is from the junction of the Castle-ton to Hutton-le-Hole road and a turning from Farndale about 1/2 mile south of the Lion Inn. The walker heads across country to Esklets along the track of the old railway around the head of Farndale. The path then runs along the Esk to Westerdale and Castleton station, and on to Danby station. The Danby Lodge National Park Centre is the next objective, followed by the ascent of Danby Beacon, 981 feet up with extensive views, and the descent to Lealholm. Now it is on to Glaisdale through woodland and farmland, then along an old paved pannier way to Egton Bridge and a former toll road to Grosmont. Then come Sleights and Whitby, where the River Esk meets the sea.

The Lyke Wake Walk

Essential Information

Length: 40 miles, from Sheepwash Car Park, Osmotherley, to Beacon Howes, Ravenscar
Going: extremely tough indeed
OS maps: 93, 94, 99, 100

This is a walk like none other. It runs straight across the main watershed of the North York Moors and is a tough walk at the best of times. In bad, or even doubtful, weather it should not be attempted. The walk must be completed in less than 24 hours: the normal time is 14 to 18 hours. Proper training and equipment are absolutely vital; and a definite schedule must be worked out and kept to, with arranged meetings with support parties. The walk should always be undertaken in a group; optimum size is five to ten people.

The route runs from Osmotherley over Live and Cringle Moors, then drops

Sutton Bank.

harply and rises equally harply to Cold Moor and Clay ʒank Top. The next target is the ighest point of the North York Moors, Botton Head, 1,489 feet p on Urra Moor. Then there is stretch on an old pack-horse rack, followed by more moorand to Esklets, Ralph Cross nd White Cross. An alternaʄive route runs via the Lion Inn. 'he halfway point is just past Loose Howe. After Shunner Howe comes Wheeldale, the oughest section of the whole ough walk, a wild stretch of eep heather. Simon Howe, ʼen Bogs Houses, Ellerbeck ınd Lilla Howe come next, ʻollowed by Jugger Howe. An lternative route from Hamer House runs further north over gton High Moor and past Sil Howe and York Cross.

The North Wolds Walk

Essential Information

Length: 20 miles, a circular route through Thixendale, Bishop Wilton and Millington
Going: relatively easy
OS map: 100

This is a pleasant walk through varied scenery in the North Yorkshire Wolds. The start is at the Huggate turning by Wayrham Farm on the A166, about 3 miles south-west of Fridaythorpe. The first village reached is Thixendale, followed by Bishop Wilton. The walker then makes for Great Givendale and crosses the Whitekeld Beck into Millington. The last section runs

Danby High Moor from Ralph Cross.

through a Forestry Commission plantation back to the starting-point.

Suggested Walking Areas

North York Moors

● Farndale

Three daffodil walks (1 hour, 2 hours and 2½ hours) start from the two car parks in Farndale. They are best tackled in the third and fourth weeks of April.

● Goathland

This 3-mile route follows the track of the original Whitby to Pickering Railway. The line was opened in 1836. At first only horse-drawn traffic used it, but after improvements steam locomotives began operating in 1847. Eighteen years later a deviation line was built bypassing the 1 in 15 gradient from Beck Hole to Goathland. The line closed in 1965 but was re-opened in 1973 as a privately operated steam line. The walk, which follows the original line, has fine views and passes tunnels and railway workers' cottages as well as descending the incline.

● The May Beck Trail

This is a 3-mile route leading across moorland and forest. The starting-point is at May Beck, 1½ miles from Redgates. Two features are four linear mounds and ditches, perhaps part of a Bronze Age settlement, and an old sheep house.

● Ravenscar

A trail runs for 5½ miles around Ravenscar from the National Trust Centre, one part towards the foreshore, the other along the old Scarborough to Whitby line to a now disused quarry.

● Sutton Bank

A 2-mile nature trail starts at the car park at the top of Sutton Bank and runs to Garbutt Wood Nature Reserve and near Whitestone Cliff.

● Other recommended waymarked walks in the North York Moors National Park are:
Rosedale Abbey circular (1½ miles)
Castleton to Commondale (3 miles)
Egton Bridge to Egton circular (3 miles)
Glaisdale to Egton Bridge (3 miles)
Rosedale Abbey to Stone Bank Crag circular (2 miles)
Grosmont to Lease Rigg and the Esk Valley circular (3 miles)
Goathland to Mallyan Spout and Incline Cottage circular (3 miles)

Yorkshire Dales

● Bolton Abbey

North of the Abbey, a path leads along the River Wharfe to The Strid, a narrow chasm through which the river races. Beyond there are paths up to

Pembroke Seat and to the Barden Bridge.

● Harrogate

There are paths from the centre to Harlow Car and to Haverah Park. Another route runs to Pannal and Burn Bridge.

● Littondale

There are superb short walks in this valley with goods views and interesting natural history. For a wild walk to Malham, climb up over Great Close from the Falcon Inn at Arncliffe, keeping Gordale Beck on the left. Walk along the Malham road about a mile south-east of Malham Tarn and then turn left along Mastiles Lane for Kilnsey. This road is restricted to walkers.

Half a mile north of Litton a green track runs across country between Pen-y-Ghent and Fountains Fell to the Settle road.

Pen-y-Ghent.

● The Three Peaks

The Dales' famous three peaks are Pen-y-Ghent (2,273 feet), Ingleborough (2,373 feet), and Whernside (2,414 feet). A tough 22-mile walk links the three, requiring over 9,000 feet of ascent and descent. The walk must be completed in less than 12 hours, and walkers should register at the Pen-y-Ghent Cafe in Horton. The walk is marvellous, across wild and majestic moorland and with wide views to the Lakes and the Irish Sea.

● Wharfedale

There are many fine footpaths in this dale, especially between Grassington and Aysgarth. Especially recommended are:
Bolton Abbey to Simon's Seat
Buckden to Yockenthwaite along the Roman road
Kettlewell to Arncliffe, where the views are stunning

OS maps: 91, 92, 93, 94, 98, 99, 101, 103, 104, 105, 106

Greater Manchester

Suggested Walking Areas

● Brabyns Park Interest Trail

A 2-mile trail running through parkland and woodland, bounded on one side by the Peak Forest Canal and on the other by the River Goyt.

● Cheadle Hulme Trail

This 2¼-mile trail from Farnham Close highlights the development and growth of Cheadle Hulme.

● Crompton Trail

This 3-mile walk from Firwood Fold in Bolton commemorates the life story of Samuel Crompton, the inventor of the spinning mule.

● Etherow Country Park, Compstall

1¼-mile trail through mixed woodland and the Etherow Valley.

● Haigh Hall Nature Trail

2 miles from Wigan Lane entrance to the Haigh Hills Country Park through woods and past a quarry, along river and canal banks.

● Hopwood Clough Nature Trail

2 miles through woodland with good views of the Pennines.

● Nob End Nature Trail

A ½-mile trail starting from Little Lever and taking in an old quarry and the junction of waterways.

● Tame Valley Nature Trails

These seven trails between 1 and 1½ miles long, cover the main buildings and architecture of the Peak Forest Canal. The first three start from Portland Basin in Ashton, the fourth from Ashton Street, Dukinfield, and the fifth from Dunkirk Lane, Dukinfield. Starting-points for the last two are Manchester Road and Woodend Lane, both in Hyde.

OS maps: 109, 110

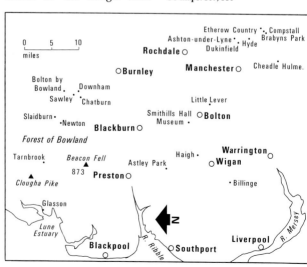

Lancashire

View south over River Wyre at Tarnbrook.

Suggested Walking Areas

● Astley Park Nature Trail

This 2-mile trail runs through woodlands with plentiful flora and fauna.

● Beacon Fell Country Park

Beacon Fell, 873 feet high, commands fine views of the surrounding area. The Park, which offers much to the walker, naturalist and geographer, is crossed by numerous footpaths, six of which lead to the summit.

● Birkacre Valley Trail

A 1½-mile nature trail around land once mined and now reclaimed.

● Forest of Bowland

This is a secluded, mysterious area, little visited despite its proximity to towns such as Preston. There are many footpaths, some in the wooded dales, others high on the fells. Among the best walks are:
Slaidburn to Bell Sykes and Holme Head Bridge
Slaidburn to Newton via Dunmow Park and along the Hodder Valley
Slaidburn to Ellerbeck via the Shay Woods
Tarnbrook to Clougha over Wardstone and Grit Fell
Bolton - by - Bowland to Downham (7½ miles) through the Ribble Valley and the villages of Sawley and Chatburn.

● Lune Estuary

A 3¼-mile footpath runs from Glasson Dock to Aldcliffe along a disused railway track.

● Witton Country Park

Here there are woodland walks, a tree trail and a nature trail. There are good views from Billinge Hill, 880 feet up.

● Wycoller Country Park

An interesting park centred on the old agricultural settlement of Wycoller, preserved as it was in the 19th century. Footpaths link the various sites and view points, which include the 16th-century Wycoller Hall, Foster's Leap, Raven Rock and Bracken Hill.

OS maps: 97, 98, 102, 103, 108, 109

135

Cumbria

The Allerdale Ramble

Essential Information

Length: 55 miles, from Seathwaite to Silloth
Going: usually easy, but with quite a few hard stretches
OS maps: 85, 89

This is a fine walk, from the centre of the Lakes through the Derwent Valley to the Solway coast. Frequent alternative routes mean that walkers who like high ground and those who prefer lower levels will be satisfied. The start is at Seathwaite, at the head of Borrowdale, and soon there is drama, for the path climbs to the top of the 900-foot Castle Crag, giving superb views of Borrowdale and Derwentwater. An alternative route keeps to the valley bottom. After Grange the way runs high above Derwentwater or alongside the banks to Portinscale, which is only a short walk from Keswick.

Yet another set of alternatives leads either up to the level top of Skiddaw, with magnificent views all round, or on the flat by the River Derwent beside Dodd Wood to Bassenthwaite Lake. The Skiddaw path descends past Long Side. Past Armathwaite Hall, the next target is Isel, where yet another choice confronts the walker The main path climbs to Kirkhouse road and then makes for Cockermouth (28½ miles) while the shorter route omits the town altogether. Now the land begins to change, and the walker forsakes mountains for the coast, reached at Maryport. An alternative route from Tallentire reaches the coast further north at Crosscanonby. From Maryport the Ramble keeps to the coastline, and the walker can follow the road, the beach or the open green Moving north towards Allonby, there are fine views of the Galloway hills. Past Mawbray Bank, once quarried but now a pleasant area of dunes, and the Roman fort, part of a coastal chain, the target is the normal end of the walk at Silloth, although officially the Ramble continues a mile or so north to Grune Point, where there are impressive views of the Solway.

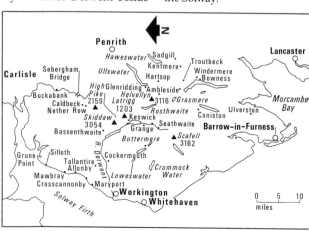

The Cumbria Way

Essential Information

Length: 70 miles, from Ulverston to Carlisle
Going: relatively easy
OS maps: 85, 90, 97

The Cumbria Way runs south-north through the heart of the Lake District, past some of its best-known waters and below some of its most celebrated peaks. By and large it is a valley walk, but none the less enjoyable, with frequent moments of splendour. From Ulverston the first objective is Coniston, reached via Newbiggin, Hollowmire and Keldray. Ahead there are views to Scafell and Scafell Pike, behind to Morecambe Bay and the Three Peaks in Yorkshire. After Tottlebank the Way climbs to Beacon Tarn, then descends to run alongside Coniston Water into Coniston. Past Tarn Hows, the path leads to Skelwith Bridge, past Elterwater (the hills ahead are the Langdale Pikes) towards Great Langdale

Coniston Water.

High Street massif from Kentmere.

and the New Dungeon Ghyll Hotel. Up Stake Pass, the walker descends again to Langstrath Valley and Long-thwaite Youth Hostel or Ros-thwaite village. Derwentwater is soon reached, and the path runs along the western shore into Keswick. The walker climbs past Latrigg and then strikes across moorland to Skiddaw House, where there is a choice of routes to Caldbeck. The direct, high-level route climbs 2,000 feet to High Pike and then descends to Nether

Row. The alternative path runs through Dash Falls and Bassen-thwaite and should always be used in bad weather or if it threatens. The paths meet at Nether Row, and it is a short walk into Caldbeck, where John Peel is buried. From here the Way climbs steeply at first, then becomes easier over Sebergham Bridge and on to Bellbridge. Follow the River Caldew to just past Rose Bridge and then make across country

...or Hawksdale Hall. After Buckabank village it is a simple straight walk into Carlisle beside the railway.

Suggested Walking Areas

For climbers and non-climbers alike, the Lake District is magnificent walking country. The high-level routes require some climbing, or at least scrambling, expertise, but the low- and medium-level walks are open to everyone.

● Buttermere

Buttermere Valley is excellent walking country, with three lakes, Crummock Water, Buttermere and Loweswater.
The **Buttermere lakeside walk** (2½ hours) leaves Buttermere by the track to the left of the Fish Hotel, runs down to the shore, up through woods and then back to the shore again. A footbridge takes the walker into Gatesgarth. Then turn left along the shore to the woods, and cross stiles to a small rock tunnel. The path then crosses yet another stile, runs alongside the beck and finally veers left via steps and a gate back to the village.

● Coniston Water

The Old Man of Coniston, at 2,631 feet the largest in the Coniston group of fells, can be tackled on a relatively easy path from Coniston village.
The **Coppermines Valley Path** runs to the foot of the Old Man. Turn right after the Sun Hotel across fields and over a bridge. Before a second bridge the path turns left along a wall to a second gate (there are good views of Coniston Water here). Now cross Mealy Gill on the stepping-stones and return to the road. Turn right into a lane, then left via the railway bridge to the road, and it is an easy ½-mile walk back to the village. The land here was once mined for copper, so take care to avoid old mine workings.

● Derwentwater

Keswick on the north shore of Derwentwater is the starting-point for a number of walks.
Keswick to Castle Head and back (4 miles). Take the Borrowdale road (B5289) for ½ mile and then follow the

Derwentwater.

path 300 feet up Castle Head, to fine views of Borrowdale, Derwentwater and Skiddaw Ridge. The path then descends to Springs Road and Springs Farm and continues for about ½ mile to a gate. Turn right to Great Wood and the main road. Cross to the lake and walk back along the shore to Keswick.

● Grasmere

The walk from **Grasmere to Ambleside** leaves from Red Bank on the Langdale Road, makes for Deerbolts Wood and then climbs up to Loughrigg Terrace. Views down to the Lake and up to the mountains are impressive. Bear right from the terrace to the old quarry of Rydal Cave and then follow the track across the hill to a T-junction, where a minor road leads down into Ambleside.

Grasmere to Patterdale is a good 4-hour medium-level walk with one major uphill stretch. The path leaves the A591 Grasmere to Keswick road a few miles north of Grasmere and almost immediately strikes towards Helvellyn. The target is Grisedale Tarn, a lonely pool underneath the towering peak. The path then winds gently and slowly downhill to Patterdale, finishing in a pleasant stretch through farmland.

● Ullswater

Glenridding to Eagle Crag and back (3 hours). Take the river path from Glenridding, a small village at the southern end of Ullswater, to Wetside. Then fork left, following signs to Keldas and Lantys Tarn. South

Walkers above Coniston.

The church at Grasmere where Wordsworth is buried.

of the Tarn, turn down to Grisedale, then up to Grisedale Tarn and on to Braesteads and Eagle Crag. There are fine views, especially of Sunday Crag and Dollywagon Pike. Now follow the path back to Grisedale Tarn and then on down to Gatterdale and Glenridding.

High Street is a Roman road that runs the length of the ridge separating Ullswater and Haweswater, from Penrith south to Windermere. The ridge path makes a fine walk and can be joined by footpaths leading up from Patterdale, the northern and southern tips of Haweswater and Hartsop. The main descent is to Troutbeck, a few miles north of Windermere, but paths also run down to Kentmere and Sadgill. The views from the top are really marvellous.

● Windermere

This is the biggest lake in England, 10½ miles long. Although it is busy and popular, the walker can soon leave the crowds behind.

Bowness Circular Walk (2 to 4 hours) leaves Bowness pier towards Cockshott Point and then crosses the lake by ferry. About 300 yards from the ferry, take an uphill path on the right. Go under the main arch of the folly and then fork left to the Claife Heights footpath. At a deer fence, the path joins an old bridleway, then veers right downhill to the shore and the ferry.

Windermere to Orrest Head (1 hour). The walk begins in Windermere village, climbs uphill through the woods and turns right through a kissing gate to reach rocky Orrest Head. The views are superb.

OS maps: 85, 86, 89, 90, 91, 96, 97, 98

141

Cleveland

The Cleveland Way (see pages 112-113) is the chief footpath through Cleveland, taking the walker over moorland and along the majestic coastline.

Suggested Walking Areas

● The Captain Cook Boyhood Walk

Cook Country extends into modern North Yorkshire, consisting of the area between the River Tees and Whitby. The Boyhood Walk, a circular route starting from Gribdale Gate car park at Great Ayton, runs through the area in which the great explorer grew up. The Walk climbs to the Cook Monument high on Easby Moor, descends Larner's Hill and follows a lane to Airy Holme Farm, where Cook spent his boyhood. The next objective is Roseberry Topping,

the distinctive natural feature of this part of the countryside. Finally, Little Roseberry is climbed and the Walk continues along the escarpment edge back to Gribdale.

● Castle Eden Walkway

This route runs for 3½ miles on waymarked paths from Thorpe station to Wynyard station along the old Stockton and Castle Eden Railway. Footpaths at each end extend it north through forestry plantations to Tilery Wood and south to Thorpe Thewles. Footpath detours can be made to the ruins of St Thomas' Church at Grindon and Thorpe Wood. The line itself is of especial interest to naturalists.

● Cleveland Hills

Walk from Eston Moor 800 feet up Eston Nab, where Iron Age settlements have been discovered, to gain magnificent views over the Tees estuary.

● Guisborough

Guisborough, one of the county's most historic towns, is the start of several walks into the Cleveland foothills or along the old railway south of the town. The scenery on the paths to Ayton and Commondale is superb.

● The Heritage Coast

The coast provides plenty of spectacular walks on clifftops and beaches. Good starting-points are Saltburn and Staithes.

OS maps: 93, 94

Durham

The Pennine Way (see pages 108-111) runs through the western side of the county. The Teesdale stretches, though tough going, are worth the effort. Part of the Derwent Walk (see page 146) is also within the county boundary.

The Wear Valley Way

Essential Information

Length: 46 miles, from Killhope to Willington
Going: strenuous
OS map: 87, 92, 93

This path is tough walking. Proper equipment is essential. Walkers should also beware of adders and of the old mine workings that dot the route. Keep an eye on the weather too, which can suddenly turn treacherous.

The Way leaves the picnic site at Killhope Wheel, and runs through Weardale Forest. Then it goes over heathland to the plantation at Wellhope, followed by tracks past High, Middle

Weardale, near Wolsingham.

143

and Low Rush and Low Allers to Cowshill. Then it is over Race Head via the Seddling Rake to Middlehope Bank Top and on to Scarsike Head. From Red Road the Way runs through open moorland over Greenmere Head, past a lead-miners' dam, to Rookhope (12 miles), where it runs up a former railway incline, and follows the line to Parkhead.

Frosterley is the next target, with a stretch on paths and tracks, with some metalled road walking. The right of way must be kept to here. The Way then runs over hilly fields and on to the edge of Pikestone Fell. Past the mines and into Hamsterley Forest, the path joins the riverside walk along Bedburn Beck to the Forest Information Centre (22 miles). Having gone through Bedburn and over fields and tracks to Witton Castle, the route leads through the castle grounds to the edge of Witton Park village. A stretch on a former railway track precedes a riverside walk by the Wear.

The last section takes the walker along the old Bishop Auckland to Durham Railway and then through fields, along the embankment and over the Wear to the Way's conclusion at the Jubilee Bridge Picnic Area at Willington (12 miles).

River Wear at Durham.

Suggested Walking Areas

● Bishop Brandon Walk

This 9½-mile footpath follows the Wear Valley from the Broompark Picnic Area to Bishop Auckland. The going is easy, through farmland and along the riverbank, past Brandon and Willington. After crossing the Newton Cap Viaduct the path ends near Bishop Auckland market place. There are spectacular views all along the Walk.

● Castle Eden Dene

There are over 500 acres of wooded valley slopes in this spectacular coastal ravine of great interest to naturalists and geologists as well as walkers. A number of footpaths start from the mouth of Castle Eden Burn at Deneholme and run throughout the site.

● Collier Wood

An attractive nature trail runs through the picnic site south of Tow Law.

● The Deerness Valley Walk

A pleasant 7-mile expedition, the Deerness Valley Walk follows the route of a disused railway from the Broompark Picnic Area along the Deerness Valley to Esh Winning, Waterhouses and Hamilton Row. An extension to Crook is planned.

● Hamsterley Forest

A number of footpaths cross this 5,500-acre forest. There is also a fine nature trail.

● Hardwick Hall

There are 2 miles of footpaths and a nature trail around this delightful 18th-century landscaped garden.

High Force Waterfall.

The Lanchester Valley Walk

Only the section from Broompark to Bearpark of this 12-mile track along the track of the former Durham to Consett railway is open at present. When completed the Walk will link the Derwent Walk and the Waskerley Way.

● Teesdale

This is good walking country, with footpaths around the spectacular High Force water-fall. Paths run to the waterfalls and Gibson's Cave from Bowlees.

● The Waskerley Way

This path runs along the Stanhope and Tyne Railway between Consett and Waskerley, with an extension to Stanhope. The railway was once the highest in England, reaching 1445 feet near Stanhope. The views over the moors are very fine.

OS maps: 87, 88, 91, 92, 93

145

Tyne and Wear

The Derwent Walk

Essential Information

Length: 11 miles, from Swalwell to Blackhill (Durham)
Going: relatively easy
OS map: 88

The Derwent Walk runs the length of the Derwent Walk Country Park following the track of the Derwent Valley Railway, parallel to the River Derwent. The area is well wooded and there is a wide variety of wildlife and flowers. Starting from Swalwell station, the route is through Damhead Wood to the 13th-century ruins of Old Hollinside Manor above Haugh Bank Wood. Then comes the viaduct at Lockhaugh, 80 feet high. Across the river are the ruins of Gibside Hall. The footpath then passes Lilley Drift Colliery to come to Rowlands Gill and another viaduct. The next targets are the ruins of Friarside Chapel, the 90-foot high viaduct at Lintz Green and Hamsterley. The last stretch runs to Ebchester, where a Roman road crossed the Derwent, then through Shotley Bridge to Blackhill.

Suggested Walking Areas

● Curry's Point to Seaton Sluice

This coastal walk goes from the car park near Curry's Point over the causeway to St Mary's Island and the lighthouse. Return along the causeway, and then take the path through Hartley Bay and Old Hartley to Crag Point. From here there are good views over Collywell Bay and Charley's Garden. The end of the path is at the derelict harbour of Seaton Sluice.

● Killingworth Nature Trail

Rich in birdlife and wild flowers, this short trail takes in the village of Killingworth, the Seatonburn Waggonway, built in 1826 to take coal from the colliery to waiting ships on the Tyne, and Killingworth High Pit.

● Penshaw Monument and the River Wear

This 3½-mile circular walk takes in Penshaw Monument, Penshaw village and the Wear. From the village the walker passes through woodland to the Monument, erected to commemorate the death of the Earl of Durham in 1840. Then comes more woodland, field stretches and the river past Cox Green to Alice's Well. There follows a superb view of the magnificent Victoria Viaduct. Then the walk returns via Penshaw church to its starting point.

● Trow Point to Cleadon

This 6½-mile quasi-circular walk has a fascinating cliff-top section. From Trow Point the route runs along the limestone cliffs to Marsden Rock, nesting site of kittiwakes and fulmars. Steps lead down to Marsden Grotto. The rest of this exhilarating walk forms a circle, eventually returning to the Rock. Along the coastal stretch come quarries and lime kilns at Marsden, followed by the coastal park developed on the site of Whitburn Colliery. The last stage turns inland, past Cleadon Windmill and up Cleadon Hill to return to Marsden Rock.

OS map: 88

Northumberland

Dunstanburgh Castle.

The Pennine Way runs through the west of the county (see pages 108-111), offering spectacular and challenging walks, especially in Kielder Forest and over the majestic Cheviots.

Suggested Walking Areas

● The Allen Banks

This is National Trust land south of Haydon Bridge. There are several pleasant walks along the banks of the River Allen, near its junction with the South Tyne.

● Bamburgh

The 3-mile beach walk from Bamburgh to Seahouses is especially fine, along wide, firm sands for much of the way.

● The Border Forest

The Border Forest National Park

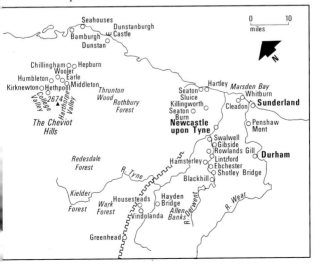

consists of the large Forestry Commission lands just below the border, including Kielder, Falstone, Wark and Redesdale Forests and the new Kielder Water, said to be the largest artificial lake in Europe. There are numerous footpaths and forest drives.

● The Cheviot Hills

The Cheviot Hills can be tough walking country, and protective clothing, plus a map and compass, are essential. There are a number of good circular walks:

Wooler to Earle Mill (3 miles) via Carding Mill Plantation
Wooler to Westwood Moore (5 miles) past early Bronze Age rocks carved with cup and ring markings
Wooler to Fowberry Mains (6 miles)
Humbleton Burn to Browns Law (2½ miles), a particularly pleasant and easy walk
Humbleton Burn to Hellpath (7 miles); the name is possibly a corruption of hill path and does not imply difficult walking

High Humbleton to Coldberry Hill (3 miles), returning via Humbleton Hill where there is a Bronze Age citadel used until beyond the Roman occupation
High Humbleton to Gleadscleugh (6 miles)
Harthope Valley to Old Middleton (4½ miles), in the Middle Ages a small village but now merely a shepherd's cottage
Harthope Valley to Broadstruther (5½ miles), into the heart of the Cheviots
Harthope Valley to Carey Burn Bridge and Old Middleton (4 miles), returning via Happy Valley
South Middleton to The Dod (6 miles)
Kirknewton to Hethpool Bell (4 miles), returning via Old Yeavering, once thought to have been the palace of the 7th-century King Edwin of Northumbria
College Valley to the Scottish border (5 miles), with excellent views into Scotland

Hadrian's Wall.

Kielder Forest, part of the Border Forest National Park.

College Valley to Red Cribs (5 miles), with a stretch along the Scottish border.

● **Dunstanburgh Castle**

A dramatic 1½-mile coastal walk from Dunstan Stead leads to the ruins of this 14th-century Castle perched on the cliffs.

● **Hadrian's Wall**

The Wall runs east-west across Northumberland. The best walk, 8 miles from Greenhead to Housesteads, coincides with the Pennine Way. Slightly south of this stretch, the fort at Vindolanda, reached by footpaths and minor roads, is also worth a visit. Milecastle 48, the best on the wall, is west of Greenhead and repays a visit.

Hepburn Walk

Three walks begin at the picnic site in Hepburn Wood, near Chillingham:
Woodland Walk (1 hour) through the larch woods
Hepburn Crag Walks (1½ hours), over moorland and past the Iron Age Hepburn Camp

Ros Castle Walk to the Iron Age fort at the top of the hill; there are superb views of the coastline and over the border.

● **Kielder**

The Duchess Drive Walk is a 5-mile circular route from Kielder Castle, up Kielder Burn and round Castle Hill.

● **Rothbury**

There is a variety of walks through Rothbury Forest in the Northumberland National Park.

● **Thrunton Wood**

Three walks start from the picnic site in the wood:
Crag Top Walk (1 hour), with magnificent views at the top
Castle Hill Walk (2½ hours), across moorland to Macartney's Cave
Farm Crag Walk, a difficult route through the hill country.

OS maps: 74, 75, 79, 80, 81, 86, 87, 88

149

Scotland

Scotland presents noticeably different walking territory from the rest of Great Britain. For the most part, access is free and open on high ground, and walkers may go where they will, with due respect for wildlife. The terrain is different too. There are numerous low-level walks, of course, and these are listed in the following pages. Many pass through landscapes of astonishing beauty: forest, wild, romantic moorland, soft hills or towering rugged peaks, snowcapped for much of the year, the lapping waters of crystal-blue lochs.

But sooner or later most walkers will look to the high ground – to the moors, hills and mountain peaks that make Scotland such a fine land. The confidence born of experience is necessary here, and walkers should not venture out alone, nor in bad or doubtful weather, nor without map, compass and note left behind giving details of the route planned.

1   Borders
2   Dumfries and Galloway
3   Strathclyde
4   Lothian and Fife
5   Central
6   Tayside
7   Grampian
8   Highland

Some scrambling is inevitable and should be expected. But while for dedicated mountaineers there are many climbs to be achieved only with full mountain equipment, walkers willing to tackle some stiff ascents and narrow paths have an enormous selection throughout the country. The walking in the southern Uplands – especially in the Borders region and parts of Lothian – is fine. But it is to the Highlands – to Highland region itself, and to Strathclyde, Central and Grampian – that most walkers turn. And rightly: for what can compare with the exhilarating ascent of Ben Lomond or Ben Nevis, Britain's highest peak, or of the many other summits listed here?

This is the culmination – actual and metaphorical – of walking in Britain.

Practical Points on Mountain Walking

Training is important. Get used to walking, even in the city and on the way to work. Eschew the lift and take the stairs!

● Basic mountain skills can be learnt and practised at Outdoor Centres and on courses or with clubs throughout the country.

● Longer itineraries should always be carefully planned, with the emphasis on proficiency and safety. Research and work out on the map escape routes from the high ground should the weather turn too fierce to proceed.

● Parties of three or four people are preferable. Walk at the pace of the slowest, avoid stringing out, especially in deteriorating weather conditions.

● Be prepared and equipped for emergencies. Carry spare clothing (warm clothes and waterproofs) and quick-energy foods such as chocolate and mint-cake or glucose and the means to make a hot drink.

● Remember the standard distress signal: six whistle-blasts or torch-flashes per minute.

● Listen to weather forecasts, understand weather signs, and learn to recognize and treat symptoms of hypothermia or exposure. Know something of basic first aid.

The West Highland Way

Essential Information

Length: 95 miles, from Milngavie (Central region) to Fort William (Highland region)
Going: variable, but generally hard
Terrain: some farmland and woodland, but longer stretches of isolated moors and a number of mountainous sections
OS maps: 41, 50, 56, 57, 64; the official guide contains a single-sheet OS map of the entire Way

The West Highland Way is Scotland's first long-distance path. Fittingly it takes the walker through some of Scotland's most majestic scenery, its highspots including Loch Lomond and Rannoch Moor, with Ben Nevis as a grand finale. It is a route for experienced walkers, and proper clothing and equipment are essential. Especially in the northern sections, there is little accommodation available, and it is probably best to carry a tent.

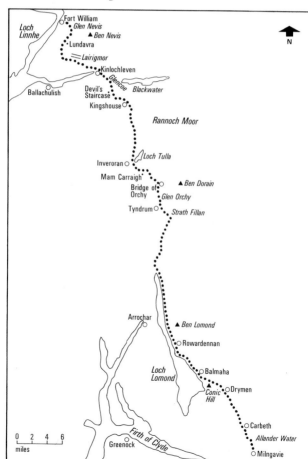

Loch Tulla, Glen Dochard and the mountains of Muckairn.

Milngavie to Rowardennan: 26 miles

The start is at Milngavie (pronounced 'Mull-guy') in the Glasgow suburbs, but almost immediately the walker is in fine, peaceful country, moving alongside Allander Water towards Carbeth. Here there are fine views north along the line of the Way. Then there is a stretch along a disused railway track to Drymen. The next target is Conic Hill, where the wilder moorland of the hills begins and the southern, more pastoral land is left behind. The eastern shore of Loch Lomond is reached at Balmaha, from where it is an easy walk to Rowardennan, below Ben Lomond.

Rowardennan to Tyndrum: 27 miles

The Way follows the Loch to its head on a surprisingly tough path with hills towering above, then alongside the River Falloch and finally on a military road, built not by the celebrated General Wade but by his successor Major William Caulfield after the '45 uprising. A pass brings the walker into Strath Fillan, from where it is a relatively easy walk through woodland and farmland to Tyndrum.

Tyndrum to Kingshouse: 19 miles

This is among the most splendid sections of a splendid walk. Running through Glen Orchy, the Way makes for Bridge of Orchy, then climbs Mam Carraigh to Inveroran. For virtually the entire way to Fort William now, the path follows the old military road, which was replaced by the modern highway as late as the 1920s and 1930s. After rounding Loch Tulla, the path makes for the wide, hostile wilderness of Rannoch Moor in a tough 6-mile stretch to Kingshouse: the weather can be bitter here, and there is no shelter at all. Eventually, however, the descent to Kingshouse does begin.

Kingshouse to Fort William: 23 miles

The head of Glen Coe is the first objective, followed by the Devil's Staircase, the highest point on the entire route, and a gentle descent to Kinlochleven. Now the walker climbs again through Lairigmor pass, rounds Meall a'Chaorainn and starts a slow descent towards Lundavra. The final stretch forsakes the military road and runs through forestry plantations, descends steeply into Glen Nevis and finishes gently at Nevis Bridge, just outside Fort William.

153

Borders

Suggested Walking Areas

● Bowhill

At Bowhill House, 3 miles west of Selkirk on the A708, there are two pleasant riverside walks of 1½ and 2 miles.

● Broad Law

It is an easy climb up Broad Law from the highest point of the road between Tweedsmuir and St Mary's Loch along the fence to the top. A 4-mile plateau runs north-east to Dollar Law.

● Craik

Two forest trails (1½ and 3 miles) run through Craik Forest from Craik village. There is a waterfall and majestic views.

● Culter Fell

There are excellent views from the summit (2,455 feet), reached by climbing the ridge between Culter Water and Kings Beck from the Coulter to Birthwood road.

● Glentress

There are four trails (1 to 4½ miles) through Glentress Forest, from the car park on the A72, 2 miles east of Peebles.

● Pressmennan

A 2-mile walk through Pressmennan Forest also runs along Pressmennan Lake and starts near Stenton, on the B6370.

● Tinto

There are good views from the top of Tinto (2,335 feet). A 2-mile path runs from Lochlyock, just off the A73 at Fallburn.

● White Coomb

From the car park at the foot of Tail Burn on the A708 Moffat to Selkirk road a path runs to Loch Skeen and up White Coomb (2,695 feet). The walk can be continued over a plateau to Hart Fell and Swatte Fell, then descending by the Moffat Water to Capplegill.

OS maps: 65, 66, 67, 72, 73, 74, 75, 78, 79, 80

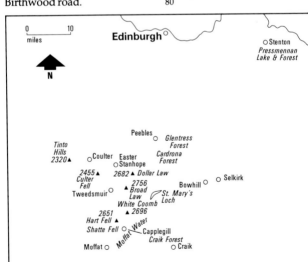

Dumfries and Galloway

Suggested Walking Areas

Ae Forest

Three forest walks (1½, 2½ and 4 miles) leave the picnic site near Ae village and run down the Water of Ae.

● Dalbeattie

Forest walks of 1, 2 and 3 miles leave the picnic site on the A710, just south of Dalbeattie.

● Drumlanrig

From Drumlanrig Castle car park the **Three Lochs Nature**

Gatehouse-of-Fleet.

Trail runs for 3 miles through pleasant woodland.

● Kells Hills

Corserine (2,668 feet) is the highest of this range of hills. Leave the A713, 3 miles north of Dalry and drive up Polharrow Burn. Then walk through the forest to Loch Harrow and over North Gairy Top to the summit.

● Gatehouse-of-Fleet

The Forest Information Centre in Fleet Forest, on the A75, 2 miles before Gatehouse-of-Fleet, is the starting-point for three forest walks (1, 1¼ and 3 miles).

● Larg Hill

Three forest trails (1½, 2½ and 4 miles) leave the Kirroughtree Forest Centre, Daltamie, 3 miles south-east of Newton Stewart, and run through woodland and by Bruntis Loch.

● Loch Trool

There is a 4½-mile trail through forest to Bruce's Stone. The start is 4 miles east of Glentrool village, 200 yards from the road to Loch Trool.

Glen Trool.

● Mabie

There are forest walks of 1, 2, 3 and 4 miles from Mabie picnic site, signposted from the A710, 3½ miles south of Dumfries.

● Merrick

This is the highest point in southern Scotland (2,764 feet). The best path is from the car park on the north side of Loch Trool along the north side of Buchan Burn through the forest, then by a dyke to Benyellary and north-east to the top.

● Stroan Bridge

The Stroan Bridge forest trail starts at Stroan Bridge car park, about 1 mile east of Glentrool on the Loch Trool road, and runs through a conifer plantation and along the River Minnoch.

● Talnotry

Three forest trails, 1¾, 3 and 3¼ miles, leave from Talnotry Caravan Park on the A712 New Galloway to Newton Stewart road. There are majestic views; the going can be steep.

OS maps: 71, 76, 77, 78, 79, 82, 83, 84, 85

Strathclyde

The West Highland Way (see pages 152-153) runs through the region.

Suggested Walking Areas

● Ardgartan Forest

There are a number of good walks through this forest, leaving from the A83, 3 miles south-west of Arrochar.
Coilessan (5½ miles) through plantations to Lochgoilhead Arboretum
Corran Lochan (9½ miles) down the Ardgoil peninsula
Glencroe (6 miles) to Lochgoilhead through Dorich Glen
Corran Lochan (7 miles) from Lettermay Farm on the B839 to Strachur

● Ardmore

There is a 3½-mile walk on forest roads with extensive views starting from the car park 3½ miles from Tobermory on the Glengorm Castle road.

● Ariundle

A 4-mile trail runs through Sunart Forest to old lead workings and a waterfall, starting near Salen.

● Ben Cruachan

The best route up Ben Cruachan (3,695 feet) is on a reasonably well-defined path west from the reservoir in Allt Cruachan via Meall Cuanail.

● Ben Ime

The path to the top (3,318 feet) starts from the source of Allt a'Bhalachain, crosses flat land north and then climbs north-north-west. Ben Ime is the highest of the Arrochar Alps.

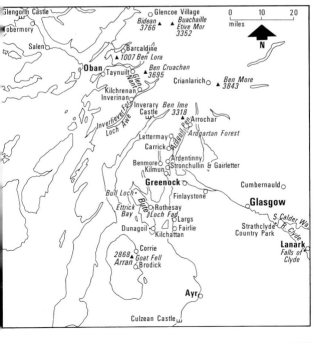

Inveraray and Loch Fyne.

● Ben Lora

A 2¾-mile walk leads to the summit of Ben Lora from Benderloch.

● Ben More

It is a tough climb up Ben More (3,843 feet) from Benmore Farm, 1½ miles east of Crianlarich.

● Benmore Forest

There are a number of walks through the forest:
Ardentinny to Carrick (5 miles)
Ardentinny to Stronchullin (3 miles)
Black Gates of Kilmun to Pucks Glen (2½ miles)
Gairletter to Benmore (4 miles)
Pucks Glen car park to Black Gates car park circular (2 miles)
Kilmun Arboretum

● Bidean nam Bian

This is the highest mountain in Argyll. There are two paths. From **Loch Achtriochtan** walk south for 1 mile into Coire nam Beith, then climb up to the west of Stob Coire to the main ridge, and follow it to the summit.

The alternative route starts at the **Meeting of the Three Waters.** Cross the River Coe and walk south-west into the Coire Gabhail. Eventually the path climbs north-west of the stream to the head of the corrie. The summit can then be reached by climbing to the col and then up the south-east ridge, or by climbing westwards to the col on the northeast ridge.

● Brodick

There are three trails (⅛ mile, 2¼ and 3¼ miles) in the country park, through the castle gardens and in farm- and woodland.

● Buachaille Etive Mor

From Alltnafeadh, 2½ miles west of Kingshouse Hotel, follow the path along a stream into Coire na Tulaich and up to the head of the corrie. There is a steep scree at the end. Then there is a fairly easy walk along the ridge.

● Bull Loch

A 3-hour trail from Rhubodach Farm at the end of the A886 on Bute runs across moorland.

● Culzean

The Culzean country park offers six walks between 1 and 4 miles, each over different terrain, and good flora and fauna.

● Dunagoil

A 4½-mile walk leaves the A844 at the junction with a side road 6 miles west of Rothesay and runs to Dunagoil Fort and St Blane's chapel past standing stones.

● Dun na Cuaiche

A number of woodland walks (1 to 2½ miles) start at the Inveraray Castle car park. There is some rough walking and excellent views.

● Eas na Circe

A steep walk for 2¼ miles through woodland starts 3½ miles north-east of Barcaldine on the A828.

● Ettrick Bay

A minor road leads from Ettrick Bay, 5 miles from Rothesay on the A844, along the shore to Kilmichael (3 to 4 hours).

● Falls of Clyde

A 2-mile walk starts from West Lodge and runs along the river gorge. Turn left off the A72

Loch Awe, Kilchurn Castle and Ben Lui.

from Lanark after crossing the Clyde.

● Finlaystone

There are trails ½ to 2 miles long through woodland off the A8 ½ mile west of Langbank.

● Glen Nant

A 2½-mile forest trail starts at Baileybridge off Taynuilt on the B845 to Kilchrenan.

● Goatfell

This is the highest mountain on Arran (2,868 feet). The paths start at Brodick Castle and at the south end of Corrie Village.

● Inverliever Forest

Forest trails (1¼ to 5 miles) start at Inverinan car park on the west side of Loch Awe on the road from Taynuilt to Ford.

● Kelburn

There is a variety of walks (½-4 hours) in the country centred on the A78 between Largs and Fairlie.

● Kilchattan Bay

A fascinating 4- to 5-mile walk around the south end of Bute starts from the old pier on the

Ben Cruachan.

B881, 7 miles from Rothesay, and runs along the shore, over rough ground to St Blane's and then over Suidhe hill.

● Locahaw Forest

This is a 1¾-mile woodland walk, running along a loch for part of the way, from the small car park in Glencoe village.

● Loch Fad

A 4½-mile walk on minor roads starts at Bute Museum on the A844, 3 miles south of Rothesay.

● Palacerigg

A 3-4 mile nature trail runs round the Palacerigg Country Park near Cumbernauld New Town. There is also a 2-mile woodland walk.

● Strathclyde Country Park

There are 20 miles of paths through park-, grass-, wood- and wet-lands, along the banks of the Rivers Clyde and South Calder Water and around the shore of Strathclyde Loch.

OS maps: 41, 46, 47, 48, 49, 50, 51, 55, 56, 57, 60, 61, 62, 63, 64, 65, 68, 69, 70, 71, 72, 77, 78

Lothian/Fife

Suggested Walking Areas

● Almondell

There is a pleasant 4-mile walk through the Almondell and Calder Wood country park on the A895 south of Broxburn, along the Almond Valley and near Linhouse and Muirieston Waters.

● Barns Ness

A 2½-mile walk starts 3 miles south-east of Dunbar.

● Beecraigs

The Beecraigs Country Park, 2 miles south of Linlithgow, offers three walks of 1¼, 1¾ and 2¾ miles.

● Cambo

A 1½-mile trail runs across farm- and wood-land from the A917, 2 miles north of Crail.

● Craighall Den

Starting-point for a 1½-mile walk alongside Craighall Burn past old quarries and waterfalls is ½ mile south of Ceres on the Lower Largo road.

● Dalkeith

The nature trails (4½ miles) from Dalkeith Town Gate pass caves and an amphitheatre and offer good views of Dalkeith House.

● Hermitage of Braid

The information centre in the Hermitage of Braid is the starting-point for a pleasant 1½-mile woodland walk.

● Hopetoun House

A 1½-mile nature trail with good views of the Firth of Forth starts off the A904, 2 miles south of Queensferry.

● Letham Glen

There is a 1-mile trail through Letham Glen, starting at the Scoonie roundabout, Leven.

● Pentland Hills

These provide fine walking near Edinburgh. A good walk is across Carnethy Hill, Scald Law, East Kip and West Kip between Glencorse and Nine Mile Burn. The climb up Caerketton from Hillend, to Allermuir and Swanston is also worthwhile.

● Water of Leith

The Water of Leith Walkway runs for 5 miles from Balerno to Slateford down the Water of Leith Valley.

OS maps: 58, 59, 65, 66, 67

SCOTLAND

Central

The West Highland Way (see pages 152-153) runs through the region.

Suggested Walking Areas

● Aberfoyle

A 5¼-mile walk through marvellous country starts at Balleich car park, Aberfoyle.

● Achray Forest

There are over 70 miles of waymarked paths in this forest north of Aberfoyle, including: **Glleann Riabhach** a 2-mile walk beginning at the rear of the Achray Hotel on the A821 5½ miles north of Aberfoyle. **Highland Edge**, a fairly steep 5-mile walk from Braeval car park on the A81 1 mile east of Aberfoyle, with good views.

● Balafuill

A 3½-mile walk through woodlands starts from Strathyre car park on the A84. There are also forest walks starting from Strathyre.

● Ben A'an

The 1-mile path to the summit is a steep climb from the car park on the A821, 6 miles north of Aberfoyle.

● Ben Ledi

The 2-mile path to the summit of Ben Ledi starts at the car park on the A84 3½ miles north of Callander.

● Ben Lomond

The path up Ben Lomond (3,192 feet) starts at the Rowardennan Hotel and climbs for 3 miles through forest and then along the crest to the summit.

● Ben Lui

There are two routes up to the summit (3,708 feet), both fairly steep. The easier path leads from the end of the road up the Cononish glen, along one of the ridges of the north-east corrie. The alternative route leads from the car park at the

Ben Lomond from across the Loch.

foot of the Eas Daimh near Glen Lochy over the River Lochy and through the forest.

● Ben Shian

Strathyre car park on the A84 is the starting-point for the 4½-mile walk through plantations to the summit.

Ben Venue

There is a steep path to the summit of Ben Venue from the Achray Hotel on the A821 5½ miles north of Aberfoyle.

● Callander Crags

The escarpment above Callander can be visited along a pleasant 1¾-mile path from Callander tennis court.

● Carron Valley

There are three short walks (20 and 45 minutes, and 1½ hours) with good views from the Spittal Bridge car park on the B818, 7 miles west of Denny and 6 north of Kilsyth.

● Glen Ogle

A 6-mile circular walk starts from 100 yards north of the junction of the A84 and A85 at Lochearnhead, along an old drovers' road, a disused railway and a military road.

● Kirton Glen

4¼-mile route along forest roads from Balquhidder church.

● Lochil Hills

The Mill Glen Nature Trail from Upper Mill Street on the A91 on the west side of Tillicoultry runs for 1½ miles.

● Wildering Forest

There are 2 circular walks of 2 and 5 miles from Leanach car park on the A821, 3½ miles north of Aberfoyle. The longer runs through the foothills of Ben Venue, the shorter along an old route between Aberfoyle and the Trossachs.

OS maps: 50, 51, 56, 57, 58, 64, 65

Loch Ard, near Aberfoyle.

Tayside

Suggested Walking Areas

● Allean

Walks of 1¾, 2¼ and 3 miles start from Allean car park 2 miles north of Pitlochry on the A9, leading to a clachan, a ring fort and views.

● Arbroath

A 3-mile nature trail runs along Arbroath Cliffs from the east end of the esplanade. Do not climb the cliffs or go too near the edge, and beware of the tides if you walk on the beach.

● Beinn Dorain

The climb to the top (3,524 feet) starts from Bridge of Orchy and runs east to the head of Allt Coire an Dothaidh and then mounts by an easy path.

● Beinn a'Ghlo

Beinn a'Ghlo (3,677 feet) is a three-peaked mountain dominating Killiecrankie Pass north of Pitlochry. Carn Liath, the smallest peak, can be climbed on a path leading from the road up Glen Fender to Loch Moraig.

● Ben Lawers

There is a clear route to the 3,984-foot summit from the car park on the Glen Lyon road, along the west side of the Burn of Edramucky and then up the south-west side of Beinn Ghlas, from where the ridge to Ben Lawers is followed. There is also a 2½-mile nature trail on the lower slopes.

● Ben Vrackie

It is an easy climb up Ben Vrackie (2,760 feet) from Moulin village, 1 mile north of Pitlochry.

● Drummond Hill

There are 3 walks through Drummond Hill Forest – of 2½, 3 and 7 miles – from the Kenmore car park, ½ mile north of Kenmore village and also from the picnic site 1 mile west of Kenmore on the A827.

● Glen Tarken

A 2¼-mile path starts at the Four Seasons Hotel on the A85 at the west end of St Fillans and runs through woodland.

● Kindrogan

The field centre here, 10 miles east of Pitlochry on the A924, is the starting-point for a 3-mile walk to the summit of Kindrogan Hill. The going is steep.

● Rannoch Forest

There are 3 walks (1, 2 and 5½ miles) through the forest from 3 miles along the road on the south side of the loch.

OS maps: 41, 42, 43, 44, 45, 50, 51, 52, 53, 54, 55, 56, 57, 58

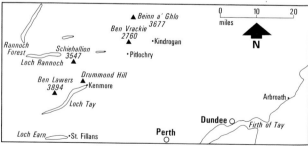

Grampian

Suggested Walking Areas

● Ben Macdui

The easiest way up this mountain, at 4,296 feet the second highest in Scotland, is to take the Cairn Lochan route from Cairngorm (see below). Descend south-south-west ½ mile before Cairn Lochan peak to Lochan Buidhe and then climb gently for 1½ miles to the summit.

● Bennachie Forest

There are a number of good woodland and hill-top walks from various starting-points:
Back o'Bennachie car park, ½ mile west of Oyne village on the Oyne to Insch road (½ to 5¼ miles)
Donview car park, 4 miles north of Monymusk on the Kemnay to Keig road (½ to 6¼ miles).

● Cairngorm

It is an easy walk up this mountain (4,084 feet), even if the walker ignores the chair-lift.

Start from the car park on the Aviemore to Loch Morlich road. In good weather, walk along the summit plateau for 2 miles south-west to Cairn Lochan and on to the end of the Coire an Lochain cliffs, then north down to the stream flowing from the corrie.

● Crathes

There are four trails (¾ to 2½ miles) through the Crathes Castle estate off the A93 4 miles east of Banchory.

● Dufftown

The Kirktown of Mortlach distillery, a little south of Dufftown, is the starting-point for a 2-mile walk, known as the Giants Chair footpath.

● Kirkhill Forest

There is a wide variety of short walks through this pleasant woodland:
Cults Wood, Dalhebity, Foggieton and Forest Lodge walks (½ to 1¼ miles), from car park 5 miles west of Aberdeen,

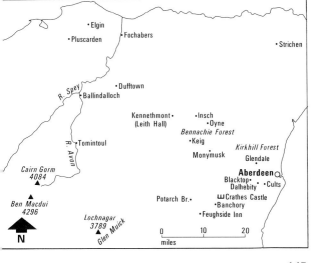

165

View from summit of Cairngorm with Ben Macdui on left.

between A93 and A944

Rotten O'Gairn (1¼ miles), on Blacktop Road, 5 to 6 miles west of Aberdeen

Glendale and Saplinbrae (¾ to 1 mile), ½ mile south of A96 junction on B979

Slacks Wood (¾ mile) on Caskieben to Pitmedden station road, off A96 8½ miles north-west of Aberdeen

Tyrebagger Wood (2¾ to 3¼ miles), on north side of A96 8 miles north-west of Aberdeen

● Leith Hall

Three trails (¾ to 2 miles) run through the estate, 1 mile west of Kennethmont off B9002.

● Lochnagar

The route to the top (3,789 feet) is from Glen Muick at the Spittal along a clear path down Glen Gelder. Leave this path at its highest point and climb up to the col and on up to the plateau. Lochnagar is the highest point of this plateau, which runs 9 miles south-west to Glas Maol.

● Monaughty

There are three woodland trails (1, 1½, 2½ miles) through woodland starting 4 miles south-west of Elgin on Pluscarden Road.

● Shooting Greens

Three fine woodland walks (1, 2 and 3 miles) with excellent views start on the road between the A93 at Potarch Bridge and the B976 at Feughside Inn.

● Speyside Way

Only the Moray section of this long-distance path is at present open, some 30 miles from Ballindalloch to Tugnet along disused railways, minor roads and through woodland. Eventually the Way will run to Glenmore.

● Tomintoul

A pleasant 3-mile walk follows the River Avon from the Tomintoul to Delnabo road, ½ mile south-west of Tomintoul.

● White Cow

This 3-mile forest walk begins on the Strichen to Old Deer road 2½ miles south of Strichen.

● Winding Walks

These walks, up to 3 miles long, start on the A98 1 mile east of Fochabers.

OS maps: 27, 28, 29, 30, 36, 37, 38, 43, 44, 45

Highland

The West Highland Way (see pages 152-153) enters the southernmost tip of the region.

View towards Glen Affric.

Suggested Walking Areas

● A'Chralaig

This is an easy climb, although steep at first, starting 1 mile east of Cluanie Inn on the road near the west end of Loch Cluanie. The path leads to the south ridge and then along it to the summit.

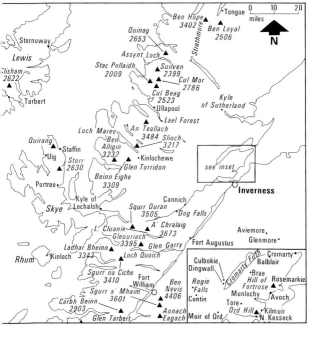

● **An Teallach**

The highest of this group of peaks, Bidein a' Ghlas Thuill, is reached from ½ mile east of Dundonnell Hotel, 10 miles north of Kinlochewe. The path runs south-east to a stream, follows it to its source and then climbs south to the peak. One corrie, Toll an Lochan, worth visiting for its views, is reached on the path 3½ miles south-east of the hotel. Follow this for 3 miles and then turn west to Sail Liath. From Sail Liath a ridge can also be followed to Sgurr Fiona and then on to Bidein a' Ghlas Thuill. Some scrambling is necessary.

● **Aonach Eagach**

There are two routes up this mountain above Glencoe: from the west end up the steep hillside north of Loch Achtriochtan to the peak Sgor nam Fiannaidh; and at the east end along the ridge above Meeting of the Three Waters to Am Bodach. These are difficult climbs.

● **Avoch**

Two 1½-hour walks start 1 mile south of Avoch off the A832, to Munlochy Bay and round Ormond Hill

● **Beinn Eighe**

Start from the ruined cottage at the foot of Coire Dubh in Glen Torridon and climb north to the main ridge, and then follow the ridge north-west to the summit, Ruadh-stac Mor (3,309 feet). Alternatively, the ridge can be gained from a path starting 1½ miles to the east, near Loch Bharranch.

● **Ben Alligin**

The path to the top (3,232 feet)

runs from the bridge over a stream 2 miles west of Torridon, heads north-west for 1 mile, climbs a corrie and turns north up open slopes to Tom na Gruagach, the lower peak. A ridge runs to Sgurr Mor, the highest peak.

● **Ben Hope**

The easy climb to the summit (3,042 feet) starts 1 mile north of the broch at Dun Dornadilla in Strathmore. A steep climb leads to a ridge, from where it is easy walking.

● **Ben Loyal**

Ribigill Farm 2 miles south of Tongue is the starting-point for the ascent. Head south-east below the peak of Chaonasaid, and then climb south-west to the summit ridge (2,506 feet).

● **Ben Nevis**

This is Scotland's most celebrated and highest peak (4,406 feet). Start in Glen Nevis at Achintee farm or at the youth hostel. An alternative and more scenic route is along the normal route to the plateau

*Left: Loch Torridon and Ben Alligin.
Above: Glen Nevis.*

halfway up, then north for 1 mile and east into the glen of Allt a'Mhuillin. Now follow the stream south-east to its source, then climb from the head of the corrie to the Carn Mor Dearg Arete ridge. Yet another possibility is to climb Carn More Dearg from Allt a'Mhuillin and then follow the ridge round.

● Brae

There is a 2-hour walk along forest tracks from Brae, off an unclassified road 9 miles east-south-east of Cromarty, past cairns and good views.

● Clisham

It is a short climb up Clisham (2,622 feet) on the Isle of Harris from the Tarbert to Stornoway road at a spot about 1½ miles south of the summit. The path runs across moorland to the slopes, where the south-east ridge should be followed.

● Coulmore Wood

Off the B9162, between Kessock and Tore and 8 miles east of Muir of Ord, there is a magnificent 1½-hour walk through woodland, with views of the Beauly Firth.

● Cromarty

At the east end of Cromarty a 1-hour walk runs along the foreshore.

● Culbokie Loch

From Culbokie, on the A9169 9 miles north-east of Muir of Ord, a 1½-hour walk leads to an artificial loch.

● Cul Beag and Cul Mor

These twin peaks (2,523 and 2,786 feet) north of Ullapool can be easily climbed via the eastern slopes.

● Dog Falls

There are 1½- and 2½-mile walks here, starting from Glen Affric off the A831 at Cannich.

● Fortrose

There are two walks here, each of 1½ hours, via Hill of Fortrose and via Mount Pleasant.

● Garbh Bheinn

Dominating Loch Linnhe, this peak (2,903 feet) is best tackled from the highest point of the Corran Ferry to Strontian road

169

via Glen Tarbert. It is a short but steep ascent. The south-east ridge offers a gentler alternative.

● Glengarry

There are two walks, of 2 and 2½ miles, to the waterfall from the forest road left off the A87 1 mile north of the junction with the A82.

Kyle of Lochalsh.

● Glenmore

Three trails run along the loch shore, one over Shepherds Hill (2,654 feet). The starting-point is on the Cairngorm road from Aviemore.

● Gleouraich

Gleouraich rises 3,395 feet on the north side of Loch Quoich. The path starts 2½ miles west of the dam.

● Inchnacardoch

A 4-mile path runs alongside the River Oich and through Inchnacardoch forest from the car park on the Auchterawe road from Fort Augustus.

● Kilmuir

From Kilmuir church, 11 miles south-west of Fortrose, there is an interesting 1½-hour walk along the foreshore.

● Kinloch

There is a 3.7-mile nature trail from Kinloch Pier, Isle of Rhum, along the Kinloch shore and then through moorland and hills.

● Kyle of Lochalsh

There are a number of pleasant walks, up to 7 miles long, around Lochalsh House on the A87 near Kyle of Lochalsh. This small town has marvellous views across to Skye and is the departure point of the ferry.

● Kyle of Sutherland

This beautiful area offers three short walks:

Drumliah, 1¾ miles from the A836 1 mile north of Bonar Bridge.

Carbisdake, a 2¼-mile route from the castle grounds on the Culrain road from the A9

Raven Rock, 1½ miles off the A837 Roachall to Invershin road

● Ladhar Bheinn and Sgurr na Ciche

These peaks, 3,343 and 3,410 feet up near the head of Lochs Nevis and Hourn, are reached by a long walk from Glen Dessary at the west end of Loch Arkaig or from the south side of Loch Hourn.

● Lael

The A835 6 miles south of Ullapool is the starting-point for a steep 2¼-mile walk to a river gorge, with good views.

● Muir of Tarradale

A pleasant 1½-hour walk runs from the B9169 1½ miles east of Muir of Ord.

● Ord Hill

There is a 2½-hour forest trail round the hill, leaving from the forest near Drumsmittal School off the B9161 north of Kessock.

Quinag

The easiest way up this towering mountain on the north side of Loch Assynt is from the Inchnadamph to Kyesku road, 5 miles north of Skiag Bridge. The path runs up to the south-western peak, Spidean Coinich, on to the junction of the three ridges at Point and then to the highest point (2,653 feet) on an easy ridge.

Quiraing

Start the ascent of this impressive Skye peak from the Staffin to Uig road and head north-west below the main line of cliffs. Beyond the Needle, climb sharply up to an amphitheatre.

Reelig Glen

There are two delightful trails through the glen, of 2½ and 1¼ miles. The starting-point is near Moniack Castle.

Rogie

Rogie Falls are reached by pleasant paths from the A832 2 miles west of Contin.

● Rosemarkie

A series of walks start from the A832 on the eastern side of Rosemarkie:

Fairy Glen (1½ hours)
Mains of Eathie (2 hours) past fossil sites
From Rosemarkie promenade there is a pleasant shore walk to Scart Craig coastal strip

● Sgurr Fhuaran

This is the highest (3,505 feet) of the Five Sisters of Kintail on the north-east side of Glen Shiel. The footbridge, which is ½ mile up the River Shiel from Shiel Bridge, is the starting-point for a very stiff climb to the summit.

● Sgurr a'Mhaim

This peak (3,601 feet) in Glen Nevis can be tackled along the north-west ridge. The mountain itself is 2 miles south-east of Achriabhach.

● Slioch

It is a relatively easy climb to the summit (3,217 feet) above Loch Maree. From the head of the loch follow the path up the west side of Glen Bannisdale, than along a stream north-west up a corrie to the top.

● Storr

This is one of Skye's landmarks. A car park on the Portree to Staffin road is the starting-point for the ascent (2,630 feet) on a path up the hillside and then up a grassy gully.

● St Michael's Chapel

Newhall Point and Balblair are the targets of a 1½-hour walk from the chapel ½ mile south of Balblair.

● Stac Pollaidh

The summit (2,009 feet) is easily reached on a path round the eastern end from the car park on the road from Drumrunie Lodge to Achiltibuie.

● Suilven

From Lochinver walk for 5 miles past Glen Canisp Lodge to the north side of the mountain, then climb the gully to the col east of the summit (2,399 feet).

● Torrachilty

There is a good 3¼-mile walk through woodland to a ridge from near Blackwater Bridge on the A832 west of Contin.

OS maps: 7-27, 31-36, 39, 40, 41, 42, 47, 49

Useful Addresses

The Backpackers Club, 20 St Michael's Road, Tilehurst, Reading, Berkshire RG3 4RP

The Camping Club of Great Britain & Ireland Ltd, 11 Grosvenor Place, London SW1 0EY; Northern England Office (Association of Cycle and Lightweight Campers), 22 Holmsley Field Lane, Oulton, Leeds

The Countryside Commission, John Dower House, Crescent Place, Cheltenham, Gloucestershire GL50 3RA

The Countryside Commission for Scotland, Battleby, Redgorton, Perth, Tayside PH1 3EW

The Forestry Commission, 231 Corstophine Road, Edinburgh EH12 7AT

The Ordnance Survey Department, Romsey Road, Maybush, Southampton SO9 4DH

The Ramblers' Association, 1–5 Wandsworth Road, London SW8 2LJ

The Scottish Youth Hostels Association, 7 Glebe Crescent, Stirling FK8 2JA

The Youth Hostels Association, Trevelyan House, 8 St Stephen's Hill, St Albans, Hertfordshire AL1 2DY

Further Reading

R. Adshead and D. Booth, **Backpacking in Britain**, Oxford Press

T. Brown and R. Hunter, **Spur Book of Map and Compass**, Spurbooks

J. Hillaby, **Journey through Britain**, Granada

M. Marriott, **Collins Concise Guide to the Uplands of Britain**, Collins Willow

M. Marriott, **The Footpaths of Britain**, Queen Anne Press

M. Marriott, **Mountains and Hills of Britain**, Collins Willow

M. Marriott, **Start Backpacking**, Stanley Paul & Co.

D.G. Moir, **Scottish Hill Tracks**, John Bartholomew

R. Aitken, **The West Highland Way**, H.M.S.O.

J.H. Barrett, **The Pembrokeshire Coast Path**, H.M.S.O.

K. Chesterton, **The London Countryway,** Constable

A. Falconer, **The Cleveland Way**, H.M.S.O.

D. Herbstein, **The North Downs Way** H.M.S.O.

B. Jackman, **The Dorset Coast Path** H.M.S.O.

S. Jennett, **The Ridgeway Path**, H.M.S.O.

S. Jennett, **The South Downs Way**, H.M.S.O.

E. Jones and R. Leek, **The West Midland Way**, Constable

J.B. Jones, **Offa's Dyke Path**, H.M.S.C.

B. Le Mesurier, **The South Devon Coast Path**, H.M.S.O.

F. Noble **The Shell Book of Offa's Dyke Path**, Queen Anne Press

E.C. Pyatt, **The Cornwall Coast Path**, H.M.S.O.

R. Ratcliffe, **The Wolds Way**, H.M.S.C.

R.G. Sale, **The Cotswold Way**, Constable

T. Stephenson, **The Pennine Way**, H.M.S.O.

A. Wainwright, **The Pennine Way Companion**, Westmorland Gazette, Kendal

C.J. Wright, **The Pilgrims Way and North Downs Way**, Constable

Acknowledgements

The author and publishers gratefully acknowledge the co-operation and assistance of the following County, District and Borough Councils, Tourist Boards and other Societies, in the preparation of the information contained in this book. They can be referred to if more detailed information on specific walks is required.

Allerdale District Council
Avon County Council
Avon Tourist Authority

Bedfordshire County Council
Borough Council of Taff-Ely
British Tourist Authority
British Waterways Board
Buckinghamshire County Council

Cambridgeshire County Council
Cheshire County Council
Cleveland County Council
Colne Valley Society
Cotswold A.O.N.B.
Council for the Protection of Rural England
Council for the Protection of Rural Essex
Countryside Commission
County Council of Hereford & Worcester

Uckfield Society
Cumbria Tourist Board

Dartmoor National Park Office
Derbyshire County Council
Devon County Council
Devon Ramblers Association
Durham County Council
Dyfed County Council

East Anglia Tourist Board
East Sussex County Council
English Tourist Board
Essex County Council
Exmoor National Park Office

The Forestry Commission (North Wales Conservancy) (South Wales Conservancy)

Gloucestershire County Council
Greater London Council
Gwent County Council
Gwynedd County Council

Hampshire County Council
Hertfordshire County Council
Heart of England Tourist Board
Humberside County Council
Huntingdon District Council

Ipswich Borough Council
Isle of Wight County Council

Kennet and Avon Canal Trust
Kent County Council

Lancashire County Council
Leicestershire County Council
Lincolnshire County Council
London Tourist Board

Mendip and Woodspring District Council
Merseyside County Council
Metropolitan Borough of Wirral
Middlesbrough Borough Council
Mid-Glamorgan County Council
Mole Valley District Council

Norfolk County Council
Northampton Borough Council
Northamptonshire County Council
Northavon District Council
North Bedfordshire Borough Council
North Tyneside Borough Council
Northumberland County Council
Northumbria Tourist Board
North West Tourist Board
North Wiltshire County Council
North York Moors National Park, Information Service
Nottinghamshire County Council

Oxfordshire County Council

Peak National Park
Powys County Council

Ramblers Association
Reckitts Rambling Club
River Foss Amenity Society

Scottish Tourist Board
Shropshire County Council
Somerset County Council
South East England Tourist Board
Southern Tourist Board
South Glamorgan County Council
Stafford Borough Council

Staffordshire County Council
Staffordshire Moorlands District Council
Suffolk County Council
Superintendent of Epping Forest
Surrey Amenity Council

Thames and Chiltern Tourist Board
Tunbridge Wells County Council
Tyne & Wear County Council

Wales Tourist Board
Wealdway Steering Group
West County Tourist Board
West Derbyshire County Council
West Glamorgan County Council
West Sussex County Council
Wey and Arun Canal Trust

Yorkshire and Humberside Tourist Board

Picture Acknowledgements

Numbers in bold refer to colour

British Tourist Authority: 16, **19**

J. Allan Cash Ltd: Title page, 21 (both), 25, **27**, 29, 30, 32, 33, **35**, 37, 38, 41, **42**, **43**, **47**, 49 (below), **51**, **54**, 57, **59**, 65 (both), **67**, **71**, 73 (above), 81, 85, **91**, 92, **95**, 97, **99**, 101, **115**, 117, **118**, 120, 121, **123**, 124, 125, **127**, 129, 137, **139**, 140, 141, 143, 144, 145, **147**, 149, 155, 156, **159**, 162, **163**.

John Cleare: 49 (above), 52, 60, 69, 73 (below), **74**, 74, 83, 109, 110, **111**, **130**, 131, 133, **135**, **138**, 153, **166**, 168.

Michael Marriott: 17, 20, **23**, 113, 148, 158, 160, **167**, 169, 170.

Derek Pratt: 93, 114

Wales Tourist Board: 75, 76, 78, **79**, **82**, 84, 87

Christopher White: Jacket photograph

173

Index

INDEX